NOV -8 2020

D. R. Toi
223 Southlake Pl.
Newport News, VA 23602-8323

Poet on the Prairie

I'm a 92-year-old ex-cowboy from Nebraska, and I became acquainted with the Badger ("The Cowboy Poet") about 80 years ago when he appeared at a youth camp. He gave me a few poetry tips, including "Your poetry is best if it captures the rhythm of horses' hoofs." I was so enthused I wrote my first cowboy poem, which won a prize at the Blaine County Fair.

— **Clark Crouch** | Woodinville, Washington

Sun and Saddle Leather, Including Grass
Grown Trails and New Poems

SUN AND SADDLE LEATHER

Badger Clark

SUN AND SADDLE LEATHER

INCLUDING GRASS GROWN
TRAILS AND NEW POEMS

Charles BADGER CLARK, *jr.*

ILLUSTRATIONS FROM PHOTOGRAPHS BY
L. A. HUFFMAN

Sixth Edition

ARTI et VERITATI

BOSTON
RICHARD G. BADGER
THE GORHAM PRESS

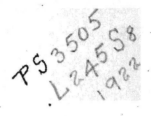

©CI.A659532

Made in the United States of America

The Gorham Press, Boston, U. S. A.

APR -8 '22

TO MY FATHER,

*who, in his long life, has seldom been
conscious of a man's rough exterior,
or unconscious of his obscurest virtue.*

PREFACE

Cowboys are the sternest critics of those who would represent the West. No hypocrisy, no bluff, no pose can evade them.

Yet cowboys have made Badger Clark's songs their own. So readily have they circulated that often the man who sings the song could not tell you where it started. Many of the poems have become folk songs of the West, we may say of America, for they speak of freedom and the open.

Generous has been the praise given *Sun and Saddle Leather,* but perhaps no criticism has summed up the work so satisfactorily as the comment of the old cowman who said, "You can break me if there's a dead poem in the book, I read the hull of it. Who in H—— is this kid Clark, anyway? I don't know how he knowed, but he *knows.*"

That is what proves Badger Clark the real poet. He knows. Beyond his wonderful presentation of the West is the quality of universal appeal that makes his work real art. He has tied the West to the universe.

The old cowman is not the only one who has wondered who Badger Clark was. Charles Wharton Stork, speaking of *Sun and Saddle Leather,* said: "It has splendid flavor and fine artistic handling as well. I should like to know more of the author, whether he was a cow-puncher or merely got inside his psychology by imagination."

Badger Clark was born January 1, 1883, at Albia, Iowa. His ancestors on his father's side were of Puritan stock and had called themselves Americans for seven generations. His mother's people were Pennsylvania Quakers. His paternal grandfather, a Vermonter, moved West in 1857 and invested heavily in a town site and manufacturing interests in southern Missouri. He was an Abolitionist and indiscreet enough to say so. The climate of southern Missouri was particularly insalubrious for Abolitionists at that period, and Mr. Clark's neighbors took such an ardent interest in his opinions that he, with his two sons, slept away from home for two months because they were expecting to be the guests of honor at a tar-and-feather party and did not care to involve the women-folk of the family.

As the Civil War drew on, the tar-and-feather threat was complicated with strong possibilities of hemp and this, with malaria, made the location so unattractive that Mr. Clark trailed north into Iowa, arriving on free soil with his family, two wagon loads of household effects, and about one hundred and fifty dollars in money.

The father of the author, after this border experience, naturally enlisted in the Union army, and served in the Western forces until disabled by wounds before Vicksburg. Returning north he entered the ministry of the Methodist church and continued therein for the rest of his active life, retiring in 1915 after an exceptionally successful and honored career of fifty-one years in the pulpit.

Shortly after the birth of Badger Clark the family moved to Dakota, which was then frontier territory, and the cowboy poet's first taste of pioneering was at the age of six months, when his mother, in the absence of his father and elder brothers, carried him on one arm while she drove a plow team and turned enough sod to save the home from one of the sudden prairie fires of the early days.

He grew up in, and with, the state of South Dakota, spending his 'teen years in the Black Hills at Deadwood. Deadwood at that time was trying to live down the reputation for exuberant indecorum which she had acquired during the gold rush, but her five churches operating two hours a week could make little headway against the competition of two dance halls and twenty-six saloons running twenty-four hours a day. This "wide open" condition of things familiarized Mr. Clark with the free-and-easy moral atmosphere of the old West, but at the same time had the odd effect of making him a teetotaler in defiance of all the older poetic traditions.

During his youth he showed no particular literary tendencies beyond an insatiable appetite for books. Luckily for his health this was balanced by an equally strong passion for outdoor life,—hunting, fishing, camping or anything of that sort, providing it was not sufficiently practical to interfere with concurrent dreaming. During two vacations of his high school course he went overland into western Wyoming and spent the summer on the ranch of an uncle at the foot of the Big Horn Mountains.

Having finished the high school with no particular scholastic honors, he entered Dakota Wesleyan University and studied there for a year. At the end of that time he was given an opportunity to go to Cuba in connection with one of the colonizing enterprises undertaken there at the close of the Spanish war, and lack of money and a romantic temperament led him to abandon his studies for the promise of a more adventurous life under tropic skies,—a step he afterward regretted. The colonization project fell through and his fellow colonists returned to the States, but he had fallen in love with opalescent surf and the rustle of warm trade winds in the palms, and so, in the spirit of the lotos-eaters and with about the same business prospects, he stayed.

While working on a Camaguey plantation a year later he had the misfortune to be present at a dispute between his employer and two native neighbors over a boundary fence in the jungle. In the course of the argument one of the natives was shot and Clark, with the usual fate of innocent bystanders, shortly found himself in irons and on the way to the *carcel*. During the two weeks which elapsed before the arrival of the cash for his bail, he spent his time in a cell with seventeen Spanish negroes and a dog-eared copy of the *Rubaiyat* handed in by an American friend on the outside.

For six months thereafter he divided his attention between plantation work, paludic fever, and a practical course in Spanish legal procedure, at the end of which time he was tried and acquitted, and then turned his face toward home in much the same mental and material condition as the prodigal son of old.

The summer of his return was spent very much to his taste, with a surveying party in the Bad Lands of South Dakota. That fall he took up an agency for a correspondence school but indifference to the charms of the business game and a constitutional aversion to dunning anybody militated against his success and he resigned in a few months to accept the city editorship of a small daily paper in Lead, South Dakota. This pleased him better, but he became too deeply interested in it and overwork, together with the after effect of tropical fever, led to a sentence of exile from his beloved Black Hills for at least two years, in obedience to which he journeyed south to Arizona.

In the cow country near the Mexican border, Badger Clark stumbled unexpectedly into paradise. He was given charge of a small ranch and the responsibility for a bunch of cattle just large enough to amuse him but too small to demand a full day's work once a month. The sky was persistently blue, the sunlight was richly golden, the folds of the barren mountains and the wide reaches of the range were full of many lovely colors, and his nearest neighbor was eight miles away.

The cowmen who dropped in for a meal now and then in the course of their interminable riding appeared to have ridden directly out of books of adventure, with old young faces full of sun wrinkles, careless mouths full of bad grammar, strange oaths and stranger yarns, and hearts for the most part as open and shadowless as the country they daily ranged.

In the evenings as Clark placed his boot heels on the porch railing, smote the strings of his guitar, and broke the tense silence of the warm, dry twilight with song, he often wondered, as his eyes rested dreamily on the spikey yuccas that stood out sharp and black against the clear lemon color of the sunset west, why hermit life in the desert was traditionally a sad, penitential affair.

In a letter to his mother a month or two after settling in Arizona, he found prose too weak to express his utter content and perpetrated his first verses. She, with natural pride, sent the verses to a magazine, the old *Pacific Monthly*, and a week or two later the desert dweller was astonished beyond measure to receive his first editorial check. The discovery that certain people in the world were willing to pay money for such rhymes as he could write bent the whole course of his subsequent life, for good or evil, and the occasional lyric impulse hardened into a habit which has consumed much of his time and most of his serious thought since that date. The verses written to his mother were *Ridin'*, the first poem in his first book, *Sun and Saddle Leather,* and the greater part of the poems in both *Sun and Saddle Leather* and *Grass Grown Trails* were written in Arizona.

He remained in the border country for four years and finally said good-bye to the desert with regret. He appears to have left something behind to keep his memory green, however, for seven years after his departure his *High Chin Bob* was discovered to be a popular song among the cowboys in a certain section of the Southwest, and was printed in *Poetry* as a true Western folksong of unknown authorship.

As Badger Clark says: "Regarding the *High Chin Bob* business, it is so far back and,

with my usual carelessness, I have neglected
to preserve any documentary evidence bearing on it, that I fear I can't give you much of
value. The thing began once when I was
with an outfit of ten men driving seven hundred cattle to the shipping point after the
roundup, acting as cook because the regular
incumbent had gone to town and looked upon
the wine when it is red. One night when I
was washing my pots and kettles I heard the
boys around the fire discussing a cow-puncher
over in the mountains who, the week before,
had roped a bobcat and 'drug' it to death.
The boys spent some time swapping expert
opinions on the incident, so it stuck in my
mind, incubated, and eventually hatched out
The Glory Trail.

"Nobody said anything about the poem,
good or bad, as I remember, and I reckoned
it had fallen rather flat until, some years later,
about three years ago, I think, a distant friend
sent me a copy of *Poetry* which featured *High
Chin Bob.* I found a real native folksong
which the cowboys were accustomed to carol
in their long rides over the romantic wilder-

nesses of the Southwest, a song like Melchizedek, without father or mother, which probably had naturally 'just growed' in the rocky soil where it now flourished. What was my amazement, in examining this literary curiosity, to find that it was my *Glory Trail,* with slight alterations, such as the omission of one line in the refrain, such rubbings down and chippings off as might happen to it in passing from mouth to mouth. I own that the 'folk-song' version is in some points more striking, and easy than my more labored original, and I believe it is better known.

"Frothingham, you remember, took it for his *Songs of Men* and I recently noticed that Rupert Hughes mentions *High Chin Bob* in a familiarly friendly way in his novel, *Beauty,* and no doubt many a country newspaper in the West has run the lines. When I was in California a year or so ago I became acquainted with H. H. Knibbs and I noticed that he introduced me to everybody as the author of *High Chin Bob.* So, under another name than the one its dad bestowed at the christening, this poem has become probably the most widely known son of its father.

"By the way, I have never heard *High Chin Bob* sung, and have some curiosity as to its homemade musical setting. If I ever meet some one who knows it, I'll make him warble it, if I have to use a sixshooter."

At present Badger Clark lives in Hot Springs, South Dakota. Recently he has learned that it is easier to talk to five hundred people than to five, and that sometimes his fellow citizens would rather hear him read his own verse than read it themselves, which furnishes a new source of pleasure in a very quiet life. He is thirty-eight years old and unmarried. He is a church member of irreproachable daily walk and conversation but somewhat uncertain orthodoxy. He never wears a starched collar and generally appears in a coat only when meteorological conditions or an occasion of ceremony make it necessary. He is six feet tall.

One who knows him intimately thus writes of the author: "Badger Clark is loved in his own home town but is not worshipped as a celebrity, for which fact, doubtless, no one is more thankful than he himself. It leaves him free to visit the public library, take part in local election squabbles, and be rated as a good citizen. He can sing in the church choir or join in the Christmas pageant as one of the grown-up children of the congregation. He is free to use his alert sense of humor, and in turn is glad to be the target for the wit of others. He can write verse on local subjects and they will be printed in the weekly newspaper and read without his fellow townsmen thinking the author odd."

The first edition of *Sun and Saddle Leather* appeared in 1915. It was a modest little volume of fifty-six pages bound in antique boards; but to prove how easily copies were disposed of, the publisher wrote this letter to the author:

"Do you happen to have a spare copy of the first edition of *Sun and Saddle Leather?* Some evil-minded person has lifted the last copy I had.

"I would be tickled to death to send you a

copy of the last edition to replace, if you are willing to make a swap."

But even the author did not have one, for this was his answer:

"I'm sorry, but my last copy of the first edition of *Sun and Saddle Leather* disappeared long ago. All I have in that line is one copy of the third edition that was so thumbed and soiléd from using it to read out of in public that it would tempt nobody to steal it.

"I suppose that I should have preserved at least one copy of the first edition for its historic interest, but, like Henry Ford, I am inclined to think that history is 'mostly bunk,' at least any sentimental tenderness over one's personal history. 'So sad, so fresh, the days that are no more.' Beautiful, but bunk, bunk, bunk. Let's rather grow tearfully enthusiastic over the fortieth edition."

In 1917 the second edition appeared. It was illustrated by L. A. Huffman, whose pictures have had their place in every subsequent edition. Back in 1878 Mr. Huffman began to take photographs with crude cameras which he made himself. These same photographs were the first of the now famous Huffman pictures comprising something like six thousand historic subjects, beginning with the Indians and buffaloes round about Fort Keogh on the Yellowstone, where he was post photographer in General Miles's army. Mr. Huffman knows his West thoroughly and his pictures help others to know it.

Having his poems run into a second edition did not make Badger Clark believe that he was straight on the road to wealth or fame for this was how he inscribed a copy:

> When my Pegasus is lopin',
>   Ory-eyed and on the bust,
> And the cares of common livin'
>   Sprawl behind me in the dust,
> And the breath of inspiration
>   Comes a driftin' down the wind,
> Then a finer life than writin'
>   Would be mighty hard to find.
>
> Just a-writin', a-writin',
>   Nothin' I like half so well
> As a-slingin' ink and English—
>   If the stuff will only *sell*
> When I'm writin'.

The same year appeared the first edition of *Grass Grown Trails.* William S. Hart wrote: "May these trails never be wholly obliterated! I love the West and them, and thoroughly appreciate anything which so beautifully illustrates and typifies it as this last volume of Badger Clark's does."

In 1919 a third edition of *Sun and Saddle Leather* was brought out containing additional poems.

In 1920 appeared a collected edition of Badger Clark's work, containing all the poems in *Sun and Saddle Leather,* all those in *Grass Grown Trails* and nine new poems hitherto unpublished in book form.

To prove that some authors are grateful, this is what Badger Clark wrote his publisher when he had seen the book:

"I am now ready to die. Hitherto I have felt that I have never done anything rightfully to prove up on my world-without-end six-by-three homestead, but now I have earned that spot of deep repose. And now I am ready for the 'Sure enwinding arms of cool-enfolding death.' I have achieved my achievement. I have done done it, as the Texanos used to say. I am the parent of a child, a real child, a grown child—no mewling, thirty-page infant in pasteboard swaddling clothes, no gas-pipe-legged adolescent looking out at the world with scared eyes that mutely beg: 'Please like me'; but a splendid, rounded-out, mature specimen of progeny, quietly elegant in garb, and bearing itself with calm confidence, conscious of the friendship and commendation of a variety of people, real people, distinguished people, people who (be it uttered in confidence) ought to know better. And I am its dad: bone of my bone, flesh of my flesh, heart of my heart, it stands and nobody can even pick out its more amiable traits and say: 'That came from the mother's side.' 'Come, lovely and soothing death,' you bleak, bloodless, black humbug, you; come whenever you're ready. I've beaten you! You can't kill me!

"Where was I? Pardon me! 'B'ar with me, y'r honor,' as I once heard a cow country lawyer say when he was trying to plead a case under a burden of emotion and mixed drinks.

But, Badger, it has taken me the best part of fifteen years to make that book and now, as I look at it, I sing to myself: 'By gosh! it was worth it!' I have stood wistfully by and watched the companions of my youth go into real estate and insurance and the ministry and medicine and standing in the world, wondering if I wasn't after all, a variegated damfool for trying to scale the perpendicular side which Parnassus presents to the half-educated. But to-night I envy no man on earth—not Rockefeller, not Doug. Fairbanks, not even Gamaliel Harding as he leads admiring millions toward the promised land of Normalcy. 'Blessed is that man who has found his work. Let him ask no other blessedness.' Why Carlyle, you dear, crusty old son-of-a-gun, you're dead right, and when I meet you beyond the last divide I'll humble myself before you for having thought, sometimes, that those words of yours were mere inspirational bunk.

"Well to return to coherency, if I can, the new Siamese-twins edition of *Sun and Saddle Leather* and *Grass Grown Trails* is really a source of some slight satisfaction to me. I have before me collections of Wilfred Wilson Gibson, and John Masefield and they, though thicker, don't look a bit better—mechanically. You've done me proud. Thank you."

The present sixth edition, we hope, will speak for itself.

Dr. W. T. Hornaday said of the book: "Some of the *Sun and Saddle Leather* poems have taken hold of me with a grip that only imbecility ever can shake loose. I have seen many poems and verses come out of the wild portions of the West; but these are the best. They are real poetry!"

Sun and Saddle Leather and *Grass Grown Trails* are Western songs, simple and ringing and yet with an ample vision that makes them unique among poems written in a local vernacular. The spirit of them is eternal, the spirit of youth in the open, and their background is "God's Reserves," the vast reach of Western mesa and plain that will always remain free—"the way that it was when the world was new."

Every poem carries a breath of plains, wind-flavored with a tang of camp smoke;

and, varied as they are in tune and tone, they do not contain a single note that is labored or unnatural. They are of native Western stock, as indigenous to the soil as the agile cow ponies whose hoofs evidently beat the time for their swinging measures; and it is this quality, as well as their appealing music, that has already given them such wide popularity, East and West.

That they were 'born in the saddle and written for love rather than for publication is a conviction that the reader of them can hardly escape. From the impish merriment of *From Town* to the deep but fearless piety of *The Cowboy's Prayer,* these songs ring true; and are as healthy as the big, bright country whence they came.

In prefaces to earlier editions I made free to quote from the poems and to attempt to point out their peculiar excellencies. With modesty unusual in authors, Badger Clark wrote:

"By the way, Mr. Badger loaded most of the odium for the biographical preface to *Sun and Saddle Leather* onto you at the time it first appeared, and I suppose you are responsible for the extended version of the late edition. It is said that modern women are deficient in spinning, weaving and other arts familiar to their great grandmothers, but when it comes to the proverbially difficult stunt of fabricating a silk purse out of a sow's ear, you are THERE. Thank you."

R. H.

CONTENTS

SUN AND SADDLE LEATHER

PAGE

RIDIN' 39
> *There is some that like the city.*

THE SONG OF THE LEATHER 42
> *When my trail stretches out to the edge of the sky.*

A BAD HALF HOUR 45
> *Wonder why I feel so restless.*

FROM TOWN 47
> *We're the children of the open and we hate the haunts o' men.*

A COWBOY'S PRAYER 50
> *Oh Lord, I've never lived where churches grow.*

THE CHRISTMAS TRAIL 52
> *The wind is blowin' cold down the mountain tips of snow.*

A BORDER AFFAIR 55
> *Spanish is the lovin' tongue.*

THE BUNK-HOUSE ORCHESTRA 57
> *Wrangle up your mouth-harps, drag your banjo out.*

Contents

THE OUTLAW 60
When my rope takes hold on a two-year-old.

THE LEGEND OF BOASTFUL BILL 62
At a roundup on the Gily.

THE TIED MAVERICK 66
Lay on the iron! the tie holds fast.

A ROUNDUP LULLABY 68
Desert blue and silver in the still moonshine.

THE TRAIL O' LOVE 71
My love was swift and slender.

BACHIN' 74
Our lives are hid; our trails are strange.

THE GLORY TRAIL 77
'Way high up the Mogollons.

BACON 81
You're salty and greasy and smoky as sin.

THE LOST PARDNER 83
I ride alone and hate the boys I meet.

GOD'S RESERVES 86
*One time, 'way back where the year marks
fade.*

THE MARRIED MAN 89
*There's an old pard of mine that sits by his
door.*

THE OLD COW MAN 92
I rode across a valley range.

Contents

THE PLAINSMEN 95
    Men of the older, gentler soil.

THE WESTERNER 98
    My fathers sleep on the sunrise plains.

THE WIND IS BLOWIN' 101
    My tired hawse nickers for his own home bars.

ON BOOT HILL 103
    Up from the prairie and through the pines.

GRASS GROWN TRAILS

THE COYOTE 107
    Trailing the last gleam after.

THE FREE WIND 109
    I went and worked in a drippin' mine.

THE MEDICINE MAN 112
    The trail is long to the bison herd.

THE PIANO AT RED'S 114
    'Twas a hole called Red's Saloon.

A RANGER 116
    He never made parade of tooth or claw.

ON THE DRIVE 121
    Oh, days whoop by with swingin' lope.

SATURDAY NIGHT 123
    Out from the ranch on a Saturday night.

SOUTHWESTERN JUNE 125
    Lazy little hawse, it's noon.

Contents

THE NIGHT HERDER 127
   I laughed when the dawn was a-peepin'.

HAWSE WORK 129
   Stop! there's the wild bunch to right of the trail.

HALF-BREED 132
   Fathers with eyes of ancient ire.

TO HER 134
   Cut loose a hundred rivers.

THE LOCOED HORSE 136
   As I was ridin' all alone.

THE LONG WAY 138
   Two miles of ridin' from the school, without a bit of trouble.

FREIGHTIN' 141
   Forty miles from Taggart's store.

THE RAINS 144
   You've watched the ground-hog's shadow and the shiftin' weather signs.

THE BORDER 148
   When the dreamers of old Coronado.

THE BAD LANDS 151
   No fresh green things in the Bad Lands bide.

THE SPRINGTIME PLAINS 154
   Heart of me, are you hearing?

ON THE OREGON TRAIL 156
   We're the prairie pilgrim crew.

Contents

THE FOREST RANGERS 159
  Red is the arch of the nightmare sky.

THE YELLOW STUFF 161
  By the rim rocks on the hill.

THE SHEEP-HERDER 163
  All day across the sagebrush flat.

THE OLD PROSPECTOR 167
  There's a song in the canyon below me.

GOD OF THE OPEN 169
  God of the open, though I am so simple.

THE PASSING OF THE TRAIL 171
  There was a sunny, savage land.

LATIGO TOWN 174
  You and I settled this section together.

THE BUFFALO TRAIL 176
  Deeply the buffalo trod it.

THE CAMP FIRE'S SONG 177
  I reared your fathers long ago.

NEW POEMS

PLAINS BORN 183
  Westward from the greener places.

THE OLD CAMP COFFEE-POT 185
  Old camp-mate, black and rough to see.

MY ENEMY 187
  All mornin' in the mesa's glare.

Contents

THE FIGHTING SWING 189
  *Once again the regiments marching down the
  street.*

THE SMOKE-BLUE PLAINS 192
  *Kissed me from the saddle and I still can feel
  it burning.*

OTHERS 194
  The daybreak comes so pure and still.

JEFF HART 196
  Jeff Hart rode out of the gulch to war.

BATTLE 198
  Do you mind that old fight in The Rattles?

IN THE HILLS 200
  *The shadow crawls up canyon walls; the rim
  rocks flush to pink.*

LIST OF ILLUSTRATIONS

Badger Clark . . . . *Frontispiece*

FACING PAGE

When my feet is in the stirrups
And my hawse is on the bust 40

There's a time to be slow and a time to be quick . 66

We have gathered fightin' pointers from the famous
bronco steed 90

The taut ropes sing like a banjo string
And the latigoes creak and strain 116

I wait to hear him ridin' up behind 142

There's land where yet no ditchers dig
Nor cranks experiment;
It's only lovely, free and big
And isn't worth a cent 168

When the last free trail is a prim, fenced lane
And our graves grow weeds through forgetful
Mays,
Richer and statelier then you'll reign,
Mother of men whom the world will praise.
And your sons will love you and sigh for you,
Labor and battle and die for you,
But never the fondest will understand
The way we have loved you, young, young land 194

XXXV

SUN AND SADDLE LEATHER

RIDIN'

There is some that like the city—
   Grass that's curried smooth and green,
Theaytres and stranglin' collars,
   Wagons run by gasoline—
But for me it's hawse and saddle
   Every day without a change,
And a desert sun a-blazin'
   On a hundred miles of range.
     Just a-ridin', a-ridin'—
       Desert ripplin' in the sun,
       Mountains blue along the skyline—
       I don't envy anyone
         When I'm ridin'.
When my feet is in the stirrups
   And my hawse is on the bust,
With his hoofs a-flashin' lightnin'
   From a cloud of golden dust,
And the bawlin' of the cattle
   Is a-comin' down the wind
Then a finer life than ridin'
   Would be mighty hard to find.

Just a-ridin', a-ridin'—
  Splittin' long cracks through the
      air,
Stirrin' up a baby cyclone,
  Rippin' up the prickly pear
      As I'm ridin'.

I don't need no art exhibits
  When the sunset does her best,
Paintin' everlastin' glory
  On the mountains to the west
And your opery looks foolish
  When the night-bird starts his tune
And the desert's silver mounted
  By the touches of the moon.

  Just a-ridin', a-ridin',
    Who kin envy kings and czars
  When the coyotes down the valley
    Are a-singin' to the stars,
      If he's ridin'?

When my earthly trail is ended
  And my final bacon curled
And the last great roundup's finished
  At the Home Ranch of the world

"When my feet is in the stirrups
And my hawse is on the bust."

See page 39.

I don't want no harps nor haloes,
  Robes nor other dressed up things—
Let me ride the starry ranges
  On a pinto hawse with wings!

  Just a-ridin', a-ridin'—
    Nothin' I'd like half so well
  As a-roundin' up the sinners
    That have wandered out of Hell,
      And a-ridin'.

THE SONG OF THE LEATHER

When my trail stretches out to the edge of
    the sky
  Through the desert so empty and bright,
When I'm watchin' the miles as they go craw-
    lin' by
  And a-hopin' I'll get there by night,
Then my hawse never speaks through the long
    sunny day,
  But my saddle he sings in his creaky old
    way:

     "Easy—easy—easy—
  For a temperit pace ain't a crime.
 Let your mount hit it steady, but give him
    his ease,
 For the sun hammers hard and there's
    never a breeze.
  We kin get there in plenty of time."

When I'm after some critter that's hit the
    high lope,
  And a-spurrin' my hawse till he flies,

When I'm watchin' the chances for throwin'
    my rope
And a-winkin' the sweat from my eyes,
Then the leathers they squeal with the lunge
    and the swing
And I work to the lievelier tune that they
    sing:

    "Reach 'im! reach 'im! reach 'im!
  If you lather your hawse to the heel!
There's a time to be slow and a time to be
    quick;
Never mind if it's rough and the bushes are
    thick—
  Pull your hat down and fling in the
    steel!"

When I've rustled all day till I'm achin' for
    rest
And I'm ordered a night-guard to ride,
With the tired little moon hangin' low in the
    west
And my sleepiness fightin' my pride,
Then I nod and I blink at the dark herd be-
    low

And the saddle he sings as my hawse paces
   slow:

   "Sleepy—sleepy—sleepy—
We was ordered a close watch to keep,
But I'll sing you a song in a drowsy old key;
All the world is a-snoozin' so why shouldn't
   we?
   Go to sleep, pardner mine, go to sleep."

A BAD HALF HOUR

Wonder why I feel so restless;
  Moon is shinin' still and bright,
Cattle all is restin' easy,
  But I just kain't sleep tonight.
Ain't no cactus in my blankets,
  Don't know why they feel so hard—
'Less it's Warblin' Jim a-singin'
  "Annie Laurie" out on guard.

"Annie Laurie"—wish he'd quit it!
  Couldn't sleep now if I tried.
Makes the night seem big and lonesome,
  And my throat feels sore inside.
How *my* Annie used to sing it!
  And it sounded good and gay
Nights I drove her home from dances
  When the east was turnin' gray.

Yes, "her brow was like the snowdrift"
  And her eyes like quiet streams,
"And her face"—I still kin see it
  Much too frequent in my dreams;

45

And her hand was soft and trembly
   That night underneath the tree,
When I couldn't help but tell her
   She was "all the world to me."

But her folks said I was "shif'less,"
   "Wild," "unsettled,"—they was right,
For I leaned to punchin' cattle
   And I'm at it still tonight.
And she married young Doc Wilkins—
   Oh my Lord! but that was hard!
Wish that fool would quit his singin'
   "Annie Laurie" out on guard!

Oh, I just kaint stand it thinkin'
   Of the things that happened then.
Good old times, and all apast me!
   Never seem to come again—
My turn? Sure. I'll come a-runnin'.
   Warm me up some coffee, pard—
But I'll stop that Jim from singin'
   "Annie Laurie" out on guard.

FROM TOWN

We're the children of the open and we hate
    the haunts o' men,
  But we had to come to town to get the mail.
And we're ridin' home at daybreak—'cause
    the air is cooler then—
  All 'cept one of us that stopped behind in
    jail.
Shorty's nose won't bear paradin', Bill's off
    eye is darkly fadin',
  All our toilets show a touch of disarray,
For we found that city life is a constant round
    of strife
  And we ain't the breed for shyin' from a
    fray.

Chant your warwhoop, pardners dear, while
*   the east turns pale with fear*
* And the chaparral is tremblin' all aroun'*
For we're wicked to the marrer; we're a mid-
*   night dream of terror*
* When we're ridin' up the rocky trail from*
*   town!*

We acquired our hasty temper from our
    friend, the centipede.
  From the rattlesnake we learnt to guard our
    rights.
We have gathered fightin' pointers from the
    famous bronco steed
  And the bobcat teached us reppertee that
    bites.
So when some high-collared herrin' jeered the
    garb that I was wearin'
  'Twasn't long till we had got where talkin'
    ends,
And he et his illbred chat, with a sauce of
    derby hat,
  While my merry pardners entertained his
    friends.

*Sing 'er out, my buckeroos! Let the desert
    hear the news.*
  *Tell the stars the way we rubbed the
    haughty down.*
*We're the fiercest wolves a-prowlin' and it's
    just our night for howlin'*
  *When we're ridin' up the rocky trail from
    town.*

Since the days that Lot and Abram split the
    Jordan range in halves,
    Just to fix it so their punchers wouldn't
      fight,
Since old Jacob skinned his dad-in-law for
    six years' crop of calves
    And then hit the trail for Canaan in the
      night,
There has been a taste for battle 'mong the
    men that follow cattle
    And a love of doin' things that's wild and
      strange,
And the warmth of Laban's words when he
    missed his speckled herds
    Still is useful in the language of the range.

Sing 'er out, my bold coyotes! leather fists and
    leather throats,
    For we wear the brand of Ishm'el like a
    crown.
We're the sons o' desolation, we're the out-
    laws of creation—
    Ee—yow! a-ridin' up the rocky trail from
    town!

A COWBOY'S PRAYER

(Written for Mother)

Oh Lord, I've never lived where churches
    grow.
  I love creation better as it stood
That day You finished it so long ago
  And looked upon Your work and called it
    good.
I know that others find You in the light
  That's sifted down through tinted window
    panes,
And yet I seem to feel You near tonight
  In this dim, quiet starlight on the plains.

I thank You, Lord, that I am placed so well,
  That You have made my freedom so com-
    plete;
That I'm no slave of whistle, clock or bell,
  Nor weak-eyed prisoner of wall and street.
Just let me live my life as I've begun
  And give me work that's open to the sky;
Make me a pardner of the wind and sun,
  And I won't ask a life that's soft or high.

Let me be easy on the man that's down;
　Let me be square and generous with all.
I'm careless sometimes, Lord, when I'm in
　　town,
　But never let 'em say I'm mean or small!
Make me as big and open as the plains,
　As honest as the hawse between my knees,
Clean as the wind that blows behind the rains,
　Free as the hawk that circles down the
　　breeze!

Forgive me, Lord, if sometimes I forget.
　You know about the reasons that are hid.
You understand the things that gall and fret;
　You know me better than my mother did.
Just keep an eye on all that's done and said
　And right me, sometimes, when I turn
　　aside,
And guide me on the long, dim trail ahead
　That stretches upward toward the Great
　　Divide.

THE CHRISTMAS TRAIL

The wind is blowin' cold down the mountain
 tips of snow
  And 'cross the ranges layin' brown and
  dead;
It's cryin' through the valley trees that wear
  the mistletoe   [head.
  And mournin' with the gray clouds over-
Yet it's sweet with the beat of my little
  hawse's feet   [blue,
  And I whistle like the air was warm and
For I'm ridin' up the Christmas trail to you,
    Old folks,
  I'm a-ridin' up the Christmas trail to you.

Oh, mebbe it was good when the whinny of
  the Spring
  Had wheedled me to hoppin' of the bars,
And livin' in the shadow of a sailin' buz-
  zard's wing
  And sleepin' underneath a roof of stars.
But the bright campfire light only dances for
  a night,

While the home-fire burns forever clear
    and true,
So 'round the year I circle back to you,
        Old folks,
    'Round the rovin' year I circle back to you.

Oh, mebbe it was good when the reckless
    Summer sun
    Had shot a charge of fire through my veins,
And I milled around the whiskey and the
    fightin' and the fun
    'Mong the other mav'ricks drifted from the
    plains.
Ay, the pot bubbled hot, while you reckoned
    I'd forgot,
    And the devil smacked the young blood in
    his stew,
Yet I'm lovin' every mile that's nearer you,
        Good folks,
    Lovin' every blessed mile that's nearer you.

Oh, mebbe it was good at the roundup in the
    Fall
    When the clouds of bawlin' dust before us
    ran,

And the pride of rope and saddle was
   a-drivin' of us all
  To a stretch of nerve and muscle, man and
    man.
But the pride sort of died when the man got
    weary eyed;
  'Twas a sleepy boy that rode the night-
    guard through,
And he dreamed himself along a trail to you,
       Old folks,
  Dreamed himself along a happy trail to
    you.

The coyote's Winter howl cuts the dusk be-
    hind the hill,
  But the ranch's shinin' window I kin see,
And though I don't deserve it and, I reckon,
    never will,
  There'll be room beside the fire kep' for
    me.
Skimp my plate 'cause I'm late. Let me hit
    the old kid gait,
  For tonight I'm stumblin' tired of the new
And I'm ridin' up the Christmas trail to you,
       Old folks,
  I'm a-ridin' up the Christmas trail to you.

A BORDER AFFAIR

Spanish is the lovin' tongue,
  Soft as music, light as spray.
'Twas a girl I learnt it from,
  Livin' down Sonora way.
I don't look much like a lover,
Yet I say her love words over
Often when I'm all alone—
  "Mi amor, mi corazon."

Nights when she knew where I'd ride
  She would listen for my spurs,
Fling the big door open wide,
  Raise them laughin' eyes of her
And my heart would nigh stop beatin'
When I heard her tender greeting',
  Whispered soft for me alone
  "Mi amor! mi corazon!"

'Moonlight in the patio,
  Old Señora noddin' near,
Me and Juana talkin' low
  So the Madre couldn't hear—
How those hours would go a-flyin'!
And too soon I'd hear her sighin'

In her little sorry tone—
"Adios, mi corazon!"

But one time I had to fly
  For a foolish gamblin' fight,
And we said a swift goodbye
  In that black, unlucky night.
When I'd loosed her arms from clingin'
With her words the hoofs kep' ringin'
  As I galloped north alone—
  "Adios, mi corazon!"

Never seen her since that night,
  I kain't cross the Line, you know.
She was Mex and I was white;
  Like as not it's better so.
Yet I've always sort of missed her
Since that last wild night I kissed her,
  Left her heart and lost my own—
  "Adios, mi corazon!"

THE BUNK-HOUSE ORCHESTRA

Wrangle up your mouth-harps, drag your
     banjo out,
Tune your old guitarra till she twangs right
     stout,
For the snow is on the mountains and the
     wind is on the plain,
But we'll cut the chimney's moanin' with a
     livelier refrain.

Shinin' 'dobe fireplace, shadows on the
     wall—
(See old Shorty's friv'lous toes a-twitchin'
     at the call:)
It's the best grand high that there is within
     the law
When seven jolly punchers tackle "Turkey
     in the Straw."

Freezy was the day's ride, lengthy was the
     trail,
Ev'ry steer was haughty with a high arched
     tail,

But we held 'em and we shoved 'em, for our
    longin' hearts were tried
By a yearnin' for tobacker and our dear fire-
    side.

    Swing 'er into stop-time, don't you let 'er
        droop!
    (You're about as tuneful as a coyote with
        the croup!)
    Ay, the cold wind bit when we drifted
        down the draw,
    But we drifted on to comfort and to "Tur-
        key in the Straw."

Snarlin' when the rain whipped, cussin' at the
    ford—
Ev'ry mile of twenty was a long discord,
But the night is brimmin' music and its glory
    is complete
When the eye is razzle-dazzled by the flip o'
    Shorty's feet!

    Snappy for the dance, now, till she up and
        shoots!
    (Don't he beat the devil's wife for jiggin'
        in 'is boots?)

*Shorty got throwed high and we laughed
    till he was raw,*
*But tonight he's done forgot it prancin'
    "Turkey in the Straw."*

Rainy dark or firelight, bacon rind or pie,
Livin' is a luxury that don't come high;
Oh, be happy and onruly while our years and
    luck allow,
For we all must die or marry less than forty
    years from now!

*Lively on the last turn! lope 'er to the
    death!*
*(Reddy's soul is willin' but he's gettin'
    short o' breath.)*
*Ay, the storm wind sings and old trouble
    sucks his paw*
*When we have an hour of firelight set to
    "Turkey in the Straw."*

THE OUTLAW

When my rope takes hold on a two-year-old,
  By the foot or the neck or the horn,
He kin plunge and fight till his eyes go white
  But I'll throw him as sure as you're born.
Though the taut ropes sing like a banjo string
  And the latigoes creak and strain,
Yet I got no fear of an outlaw steer
  And I'll tumble him on the plain.

  For a man is a man, but a steer is a beast,
    And the man is the boss of the herd,
  And each of the bunch, from the biggest
    to least,
    Must come down when he says the
    word.

When my leg swings 'cross on an outlaw
    hawse
  And my spurs clinch into his hide,
He kin r'ar and pitch over hill and ditch,
  But wherever he goes I'll ride.
Let 'im spin and flop like a crazy top
  Or flit like a wind-whipped smoke,
But he'll know the feel of my rowelled heel
  Till he's happy to own he's broke.

For a man is a man and a hawse is a brute,
  And the hawse may be prince of his
    clan
But he'll bow to the bit and the steel-shod
    boot
And own that his boss is the man.

When the devil at rest underneath my vest
  Gets up and begins to paw
And my hot tongue strains at its bridle reins,
  Then I tackle the real outlaw.
When I get plumb riled and my sense goes
    wild
  And my temper is fractious growed,
If he'll hump his neck just a triflin' speck,
  Then it's dollars to dimes I'm throwed.

  For a man is a man, but he's partly a
    beast.
    He kin brag till he makes you deaf,
  But the one lone brute, from the west to the
    east,
    That he kain't quite break is himse'f.

THE LEGEND OF BOASTFUL BILL

At a roundup on the Gily,
  One sweet mornin' long ago,
Ten of us was throwed right freely
  By a hawse from Idaho.
And we thought he'd go a-beggin'
  For a man to break his pride
Till, a-hitchin' up one leggin',
  Boastful Bill cut loose and cried—

> *"I'm a on'ry proposition for to hurt;*
> *I fulfill my earthly mission with a*
> *   quirt;*
> *I kin ride the highest liver*
> *'Tween the Gulf and Powder River,*
> *And I'll break this thing as easy as I'd*
> *   flirt."*

So Bill climbed the Northern Fury
  And they mangled up the air
Till a native of Missouri
  Would have owned his brag was fair.
Though the plunges kep' him reelin'
  And the wind it flapped his shirt,
Loud above the hawse's squealin'
  We could hear our friend assert

"I'm the one to take such rakin's as a
joke.
Some one hand me up the makin's of
a smoke!
If you think my fame needs
bright'nin'
W'y I'll rope a streak of lightnin'
And I'll cinch 'im up and spur 'im till
he's broke."

Then one caper of repulsion
  Broke that hawse's back in two.
Cinches snapped in the convulsion;
  Skyward man and saddle flew.
Up he mounted, never laggin',
  While we watched him through our
  tears,
And his last thin bit of braggin'
  Came a-droppin' to our ears.

"If you'd ever watched my habits very
close
You would know I've broke such rab-
bits by the gross.

I have kep' my talent hidin';
I'm too good for earthly ridin'
And I'm off to bust the lightnin's,—
    Adios!"

Years have gone since that ascension.
    Boastful Bill ain't never lit,
So we reckon that he's wrenchin'
    Some celestial outlaw's bit.
When the night rain beats our slickers
    And the wind is swift and stout
And the lightnin' flares and flickers,
    We kin sometimes hear him shout—

    "I'm a bronco-twistin' wonder on the
        fly;
    I'm the ridin' son-of-thunder of the sky.
      Hi! you earthlin's, shut your win-
        ders
      While we're rippin' clouds to flind-
        ers.
      If this blue-eyed darlin' kicks at you,
        you die!"

Stardust on his chaps and saddle,
    Scornful still of jar and jolt,

He'll come back some day, astraddle
  Of a bald-faced thunderbolt.
And the thin-skinned generation ·
  Of that dim and distant day
Sure will stare with admiration
  When they hear old Boastful say—

> *"I was first, as old rawhiders all con-
>   fessed.*
> *Now I'm last of all rough riders, and
>   the best.*
> * Huh, you soft and dainty floaters,*
> * With your a'roplanes and motors —*
> * Huh! are you the great grandchildren
>   of the West!"*

THE TIED MAVERICK

Lay on the iron! the tie holds fast
  And my wild record closes.
This maverick is down at last
  Just roped and tied with roses.
And one small girl's to blame for it,
Yet I don't fight with shame for it—
Lay on the iron; I'm game for it,
  Just roped and tied with roses.

I loped among the wildest band
  Of saddle-hatin' winners—
Gay colts that never felt a brand
  And scarred old outlaw sinners.
The wind was rein and guide to us;
The world was pasture wide to us
And our wild name was pride to us—
  High headed bronco sinners!

So, loose and light we raced and fought
  And every range we tasted,
But now, since I'm corralled and caught,
  I know them days were wasted.

© Huttman-Stevenson.

"There's a time to be slow and a time to be quick."

See page 43

From now, the all-day gait for me,
The trail that's hard but straight for me,
For down that trail, who'll wait for me!
  Ay! them old days were wasted!

But though I'm broke, I'll never be
  A saddle-marked old groaner,
For never worthless bronc like me
  Got such a gentle owner.
There could be colt days glad as mine
Or outlaw runs as mad as mine
Or rope-flung falls as bad as mine,
  But never such an owner.

Lay on the iron, and lay it red!
  I'll take it kind and clever.
Who wouldn't hold a prouder head
  To wear that mark forever?
I'll never break and stray from her;
I'd starve and die away from her.
Lay on the iron—it's play from her—
  And brand me hers forever!

A ROUNDUP LULLABY

Desert blue and silver in the still moonshine,
  Coyote yappin' lazy on the hill,
Sleepy winks of lightnin' down the far sky
    line,
  Time for millin' cattle to be still.

> *So—o, now, the lightnin's far away,*
>   *The coyote's nothin' skeery;*
>   *He's singin' to his dearie—*
> *Hee—ya, tammalalleday!*
>   *Settle down, you cattle, till the mornin'.*

Nothin' out the hazy range that you folks
    need,
  Nothin' we kin see to take your eye.
Yet we got to watch you or you'd all stam-
    pede,
  Plungin' down some royo bank to die.

> *So—o, now, for still the shadows stay;*
>   *The moon is slow and steady;*
>   *The sun comes when he's ready.*
> *Hee—ya, tammalalleday!*
>   *No use runnin' out to meet the mornin'.*

Cows and men are foolish when the light
    grows dim,
  Dreamin' of a land too far to see.
There, you dream, is wavin' grass and streams
    that brim
  And it often seems the same to me.

    So—o, now, for dreams they never pay.
    The dust it keeps us blinkin',
    We're seven miles from drinkin'.
    Hee—ya, tammalalleday!
    But we got to stand it till the mornin'.

Mostly it's a moonlight world our trail winds
    through.
  Kain't see much beyond our saddle horns.
Always far away is misty silver-blue;
  Always underfoot it's rocks and thorns.

    So—o, now. It must be this away—
    The lonesome owl a-callin',
    The mournful coyote squallin'.
    Hee—ya, tammalalleday!
    Mocking-birds don't sing until the
      mornin'.

Always seein' 'wayoff dreams of silver-blue,
  Always feelin' thorns that stab and sting.
Yet stampedin' never made a dream come
      true,
  So I ride around myself and sing,

  So—o, now, a man has got to stay,
    A-likin' or a-hatin',
    But workin' on and waitin'.
  Hee—ya, tammalalleday!
    All of us are waitin' for the mornin'.

THE TRAIL O' LOVE

My love was swift and slender
  As an antelope at play,
And her eyes were gray and tender
  As the east at break o' day,
And I sure was shaky hearted
  And her flower face was pale
On that silver night we parted,
  When I sang along the trail:

> *Forever—forever —*
>   *Oh, moon above the pine,*
> *Like the matin' birds in Springtime,*
>   *I will twitter while you shine.*
> *Rich as ore with gold a-glowin',*
> *Sweet as sparklin' springs a-flowin',*
> *Strong as redwoods ever growin',*
>   *So will be this love o' mine.*

I rode across the river
  And beyond the far divide,
Till the echo of "forever"
  Staggered faint behind and died.

For the long trail smiled and beckoned
  And the free wind blowed so sweet,
That life's gayest tune, I reckoned,
  Was my hawse's ringin' feet.

    Forever—forever—
      Oh, stars, look down and sigh,
    For a poison spring will sparkle
      And the trustin' drinker die.
    And a rovin' bird will twitter
    And a worthless rock will glitter
    And a maiden's love is bitter
      When the man's is proved a lie.

Last the rover's circle guidin'
  Brought me where I used to be,
And I met her, gaily ridin'
  With a smarter man than me.
Then I raised my dusty cover
  But she didn't see nor hear,
So I hummed the old tune over,
 , Laughin' in my hawse's ear:

    Forever—forever—
      Oh, sun, look down and smile

If the snowflake specks the desert
  Or the yucca blooms awhile.
Ay! what gloom the mountain covers
Where the driftin' clouds shade hov-
    ers!
Ay! the trail o' parted lovers,
  Where "forever" lasts a mile!

BACHIN'

Our lives are hid; our trails are strange;
  We're scattered through the West
In canyon cool, on blistered range
  Or windy mountain crest.
Wherever Nature drops her ears
  And bares her claws to scratch,
From Yuma to the north frontiers,
  You'll likely find the bach',
      You will,
  The shy and sober bach'!

Our days are sun and storm and mist,
  The same as any life,
Except that in our trouble list
  We never count a wife.
Each has a reason why he's lone,
  But keeps it 'neath his hat;
Or, if he's got to tell some one,
  Confides it to his cat,
      He does,
  Just tells it to his cat.

We're young or old or slow or fast,
   But all plumb versatyle.
The mighty bach' that fires the blast
   Kin serve up beans in style.
The bach' that ropes the plungin' cows
   Kin mix the biscuits true—
We earn our grub by drippin' brows
   And cook it by 'em too,
      We do,
   We cook it by 'em too.

We like to breathe unbranded air,
   Be free of foot and mind,
And go or stay, or sing or swear,
   Whichever we're inclined.
An appetite, a conscience clear,
   A pipe that's rich and old
Are loves that always bless and cheer
   And never cry nor scold,
      They don't.
   They never cry nor scold.

Old Adam bached some ages back
   And smoked his pipe so free,

A-loafin' in a palm-leaf shack
 Beneath a mango tree.
He'd best have stuck to bachin' ways,
 And scripture proves the same,
For Adam's only happy days
 Was 'fore the woman came,
  They was,
 All 'fore the woman came.

THE GLORY TRAIL

(*High-Chin Bob*)

'Way high up the Mogollons,
  Among the mountain tops,
A lion cleaned a yearlin's bones
  And licked his thankful chops,
When on the picture who should ride,
  A-trippin' down a slope,
But High-Chin Bob, with sinful pride
  And mav'rick hungry rope.

  "Oh, glory be to me," says he,
    "And fame's unfadin' flowers!
  All meddlin' hands are far away;
  I ride my good top-hawse today
  And I'm top-rope of the Lazy J—
    Hi! kitty cat, you're ours!"

That lion licked his paw so brown
  And dreamed soft dreams of veal—
And then the circlin' loop sung down
  And roped him 'round his meal.
He yowled quick fury to the world
  Till all the hills yelled back;

The top-hawse gave a snort and whirled
  And Bob caught up the slack.

> *"Oh, glory be to me," laughs he.*
>   *"We hit the glory trail.*
> *No human man as I have read*
> *Darst loop a ragin' lion's head,*
> *Nor ever hawse could drag one dead*
>   *Until we told the tale."*

'Way high up the Mogollons
  That top-hawse done his best,
Through whippin' brush and rattlin' stones,
  From canyon-floor to crest.
But ever when Bob turned and hoped
  A limp remains to find,
A red-eyed lion, belly roped
  But healthy, loped behind.

> *"Oh, glory be to me," grunts he.*
>   *"This glory trail is rough,*
> *Yet even till the Judgment Morn*
> *I'll keep this dally 'round the horn,*
> *For never any hero born*
>   *Could stoop to holler: ' 'Nuff!' "*

Three suns had rode their circle home
   Beyond the desert's rim,
And turned their star-herds loose to roam
   The ranges high and dim;
Yet up and down and 'round and 'cross
   Bob pounded, weak and wan,
For pride still glued him to his hawse
   And glory drove him on.

"Oh, glory be to me," sighs he.
"He kain't be drug to death,
But now I know beyond a doubt
Them heroes I have read about
Was only fools that stuck it out
To end of mortal breath."

'Way high up the Mogollons
   A prospect man did swear
That moon dreams melted down his bones
   And hoisted up his hair:
A ribby cow-hawse thundered by,
   A lion trailed along,
A rider, ga'nt but chin on high,
   Yelled out a crazy song.

"Oh, glory be to me!" cries he,
  "And to my noble noose!
Oh, stranger, tell my pards below
I took a rampin' dream in tow,
And if I never lay him low,
  I'll never turn him loose!"

BACON

You're salty. and greasy and smoky as sin
  But of all grub we love you the best.
You stuck to us closer than nighest of kin
  And helped us win out in the West,
You froze with us up on the Laramie trail;
  You sweat with us down at Tucson;
When Injun was painted and white man was
    pale
You nerved us to grip our last chance by the
    tail
  And load up our Colts and hang on.

You've sizzled by mountain and mesa and
    plain
  Over campfires of sagebrush and oak;
The breezes that blow from the Platte to the
    main
  Have carried your savory smoke.
You're friendly to miner or puncher or priest;
  You're as good in December as May;
You always came in when the fresh meat had
    ceased

And the rough course of empire to westward
        was greased
  By the bacon we fried on the way.

We've said that you weren't fit for white men
        to eat
  And your virtues we often forget.
We've called you by names that I darsn't
        repeat,
  But we love you and swear by you yet.
Here's to you, old bacon, fat, lean streak and
        rin',
  All the westerners join in the toast,
From mesquite and yucca to sagebrush and
        pine,
From Canada down to the Mexican Line,
  From Omaha out to the coast!

THE LOST PARDNER

I ride alone and hate the boys I meet.
  Today, some way, their laughin' hurts me
    so.
I hate the mockin'-birds in the mesquite—
  And yet I liked 'em just a week ago.
I hate the steady sun that glares, and glares!
  The bird songs make me sore.
I seem the only thing on earth that cares
  'Cause Al ain't here no more!

'Twas just a stumblin' hawse, a tangled spur—
  And, when I raised him up so limp and
    weak,
One look before his eyes begun to blur
  And then—the blood that wouldn't let 'im
    speak!
And him so strong, and yet so quick he died,
  And after year on year
When we had always trailed it side by side,
  He went—and left me here!

We loved each other in the way men do
    And never spoke about it, Al and me,
But we both *knowed,* and knowin' it so true
    Was more than any woman's kiss could be.
We knowed—and if the way was smooth or
        rough,
    The weather shine or pour,
While I had him the rest seemed good
        enough—
    But he ain't here no more!

What is there out beyond the last divide?
    Seems like that country must be cold and
        dim.
He'd miss the sunny range he used to ride,
    And he'd miss me, the same as I do him.
It's no use thinkin'—all I'd think or say
    Could never make it clear.
Out that dim trail that only leads one way
    He's gone—and left me here!

The range is empty and the trails are blind,
    And I don't seem but half myself today.
I wait to hear him ridin' up behind

And feel his knee rub mine the good old
way.
He's dead—and what that means no man kin
tell.
Some call it "gone before."
Where? I don't know, but God! I know
so well
That he ain't here no more!

GOD'S RESERVES

One time, 'way back where the year marks
    fade,
  God said: "I see I must lose my West,
The prettiest part of the world I made,
  The place where I've always come to rest,
For the White Man grows till he fights for
    bread
And he begs and prays for a chance to spread.

"Yet I won't give all of my last retreat;
  I'll help him to fight his long trail through,
But I'll keep some land from his field and
    street
  The way that it was when the world was
    new.
He'll cry for it all, for that's his way,
And yet he may understand some day."

And so, from the painted Bad Lands, 'way
  To the sun-beat home of the 'Pache kin,
God stripped some places to sand and clay
  And dried up the beds where the streams
    had been.

He marked His reserves with these plain
    signs
And stationed His rangers to guard the lines.
Then the White Man came, as the East
    growed old,
  And blazed his trail with the wreck of war.
He riled the rivers to hunt for gold
  And found the stuff he was lookin' for;
Then he trampled the Injun trails to ruts
And gnashed through the hills with railroad
    cuts.

He flung out his barb-wire fences wide
  And plowed up the ground where the grass
    was high.
He stripped off the trees from the mountain
    side
  And ground out his ore where the streams
    run by,
Till last came the cities, with smoke and roar,
And the White Man was feelin' at home once
    more.

But Barrenness, Loneliness, suchlike things

That gall and grate on the White Man's
    nerves,
Was the rangers that camped by the bitter
    springs
And guarded the lines of God's reserves.
So the folks all shy from the desert land,
'Cept mebbe a few that kin understand.

There the world's the same as the day 'twas
    new,
    With the land as clean as the smokeless sky
And never a noise as the years have flew,
    But the sound of the warm wind driftin' by;
And there, alone, with the man's world far,
There's a chance to think who you really are.

And over the reach of the desert bare,
    When the sun drops low and the day wind
        stills,
Sometimes you kin almost see Him there,
    As He sits alone on the blue-gray hills,
A-thinkin' of things that's beyond our ken
And restin' Himself from the noise of men.

THE MARRIED MAN

There's an old pard of mine that sits by his
    door
  And watches the evenin' skies.
He's sat there a thousand evenin's before
  And I reckon he will till he dies.
El pobre! * I reckon he will till he dies,
  And hear through the dim, quiet air
Far cattle that call and the crickets that cheep
And his woman a-singin' a kid to sleep
  And the creak of her rockabye chair.

Once we made camp where the last light
    would fail
  And the east wasn't white till we'd start,
But now he is deaf to the call of the trail
  And the song of the restless heart.
El pobre! the song of the restless heart
  That you hear in the wind from the dawn!
He's left it, with all the good, free-footed
    things,
For a slow little song that a tired woman sings
  And a smoke when his dry day is gone.

* *"El pobre," Spanish, "Poor fellow."*

I've rode in and told him of lands that were
     strange,
  Where I'd drifted from glory to dread.
He'd tell me the news of his little old range
  And the cute things his kid had said!
El pobre! the cute things his kid had said!
  And the way six-year Billy could ride!
And the dark would creep in from the gray
     chaparral
And the woman would hum, while I pitied
     my pal
  And thought of him like he had died.

He rides in old circles and looks at old sights
  And his life is as flat as a pond.
He loves the old skyline he watches of nights
  And he don't seem to care for beyond.
El pobre! he don't seem to dream of beyond,
  Nor the room he could find, there, for joy.
"Ain't you ever oneasy?" says I one day.
But he only just smiled in a pityin' way
  While he braided a quirt for his boy.

He preaches that I orter fold up my wings
  And that even wild geese find a nest.

"We have gathered fightin' pointers from the famous bronco steed."

See page 48

That "woman" and "wimmen" are different
    things
    And a saddle nap isn't a rest.
El pobre! he's more for the shade and the rest
    And he's less for the wind and the fight,
Yet out in strange hills, when the blue shad-
    ows rise
And I'm tired from the wind and the sun in
    my eyes,
    I wonder, sometimes, if he's right.

I've courted the wind and I've followed her
    free
    From the snows that the low stars have
    kissed
To the heave and the dip of the wavy old sea,
    Yet I reckon there's somethin' I've missed.
El pobre! Yes, mebbe there's somethin' I've
    missed,
    And it mebbe is more than I've won—
Just a door that's my own, while the cool
    shadows creep,
And a woman a-singin' my kid to sleep
    When I'm tired from the wind and the sun.

THE OLD COW MAN

I rode across a valley range
  I hadn't seen for years.
The trail was all so spoilt and strange
  It nearly fetched the tears.
I had to let ten fences down
  (The fussy lanes ran wrong)
And each new line would make me frown
  And hum a mournin' song.

*   Oh, it's squeak! squeak! squeak!*
*   Hear 'em stretchin' of the wire!*
*   The nester brand is on the land;*
*   I reckon I'll retire,*
*   While progress toots her brassy horn*
*   And makes her motor buzz,*
*   I thank the Lord I wasn't born*
*   No later than I was.*

'Twas good to live when all the sod,
  Without no fence nor fuss,
Belonged in pardnership to God,
  The Gover'ment and us.

With skyline bounds from east to west
   And room to go and come,
I loved my fellow man the best
   When he was scattered some.

> *Oh, it's squeak! squeak! squeak!*
>   *Close and closer cramps the wire.*
> *There's hardly play to back away*
>   *And call a man a liar.*
> *Their house has locks on every door;*
>   *Their land is in a crate.*
> *These ain't the plains of God no more,*
>   *They're only real estate.*

There's land where yet no ditchers dig
   Nor cranks experiment;
It's only lovely, free and big
   And isn't worth a cent.
I pray that them who come to spoil
   May wait till I am dead
Before they foul that blessed soil
   With fence and cabbage head.

> *Yet it's squeak! squeak! squeak!*
>   *Far and farther crawls the wire.*

To crowd and pinch another inch
  Is all their heart's desire.
The world is overstocked with men
  And some will see the day
When each must keep his little pen,
  But I'll be far away.

When my old soul hunts range and rest
  Beyond the last divide,
Just plant me in some stretch of West
  That's sunny, lone and wide.
Let cattle rub my tombstone down
  And coyotes mourn their kin,
Let hawses paw and tromp the moun'
  But don't you fence it in!

Oh, it's squeak! squeak! squeak!
  And they pen the land with wire.
They figure fence and copper cents
  Where we laughed 'round the fire.
Job cussed his birthday, night and morn,
  In his old land of Uz,
But I'm just glad I wasn't born
  no later than I was!

THE PLAINSMEN

Men of the older, gentler soil,
   Loving the things that their fathers
      wrought—
Worn old fields of their fathers' toil,
   Scarred old hills where their fathers
      fought—
Loving their land for each ancient trace,
Like a mother dear for her wrinkled face,
   Such as they never can understand
   The way we have loved you, young, young
      land!

Born of a free, world-wandering race,
   Little we yearned o'er an oft-turned sod.
What did we care for the fathers' place,
   Having ours fresh from the hand of God?
Who feared the strangeness or wiles of you
When from the unreckoned miles of you,
   Thrilling the wind with a sweet command,
   Youth unto youth called, young, young
      land?

North, where the hurrying seasons changed
　　Over great gray plains where the trails lay
　　　　long,
Free as the sweeping Chinook we ranged,
　　Setting our days to a saddle song.
Through the icy challenge you flung to us,
Through your shy Spring kisses that clung
　　　　to us,
　　Following far as the rainbow spanned,
　　Fiercely we wooed you, young, young land!

South, where the sullen black mountains
　　　　guard
　　Limitless, shimmering lands of the sun,
Over blinding trails where the hoofs rang
　　　　hard,
　　Laughing or cursing, we rode and won.
Drunk with the virgin white fire of you,
Hotter than thirst was desire of you;
　　Straight in our faces you burned your
　　　　brand,
　　Marking your chosen ones, young, young
　　　　land.

When did we long for the sheltered gloom
　Of the older game with its cautious odds?
Gloried we always in sun and room,
　　Spending our strength like the younger
　　　gods.
By the wild sweet ardor that ran in us,
By the pain that tested the man in us,
　By the shadowy springs and the glaring
　ʹ sand,
　You were our true-love, young, young land.

When the last free trail is a prime, fenced lane
　And our graves grow weeds through for-
　　getful Mays,
Richer and statelier then you'll reign,
　Mother of men whom the world will
　　praise.
And your sons will love you and sigh for you,
Labor and battle and die for you,
　But never the fondest will understand
　The way we have loved you, young, young
　　land.

THE WESTERNER

My fathers sleep on the sunrise plains,
   And each one sleeps alone.
Their trails may dim to the grass and rains,
   For I choose to make my own.
I lay proud claim to their blood and name,
   But I lean on no dead kin;
My name is mine, for the praise or scorn,
'And the world began when I was born
   And the world is mine to win.

They built high towns on their old log sills,
   Where the great, slow rivers gleamed,
But with new, live rock from the savage hills
   I'll build as they only dreamed.
The smoke scarce dies where the trail camp
     lies,
   Till the rails glint down the pass;
The desert springs into fruit and wheat
And I lay the stones of a solid street
   Over yesterday's untrod grass.

I waste no thought on my neighbor's birth
　　Or the way he makes his prayer.
I grant him a white man's room on earth
　　If his game is only square.
While he plays it straight I'll call him mate;
　　If he cheats I drop him flat.
Old class and rank are a wornout lie,
For all clean men are as good as I,
　　And a king is only that.

I dream no dreams of a nurse-maid state
　　That will spoon me out my food.
A stout heart sings in the fray with fate
　　And the shock and sweat are good.
From noon to noon all the earthly boon
　　That I ask my God to spare
Is a little daily bread in store,
With the room to fight the strong for more,
　　And the weak shall get their share.

The sunrise plains are a tender haze
　　And the sunset seas are gray,
But I stand here, where the bright skies blaze
　　Over me and the big today.

What good to me is a vague "maybe"
  Or a mournful "might have been,"
For the sun wheels swift from morn to morn
And the world began when I was born
  And the world is mine to win.

THE WIND IS BLOWIN'

My tired hawse nickers for his own home
    bars;
  A hoof clicks out a spark.
The dim creek flickers to the lonesome stars;
  The trail twists down the dark.
The ridge pines whimper to the pines below.
The wind is blowin' and I want you so.

The birch has yellowed since I saw you last,
  The Fall haze blued the creeks,
The big pine bellowed as the snow swished
    past,
  But still, above the peaks,
The same stars twinkle that we used to know.
The wind is blowin' and I want you so.

The stars up yonder wait the end of time
  But earth fires soon go black.
I trip and wander on the trail I climb—
  A fool who will look back
To glimpse a fire dead a year ago.
The wind is blowin' and I want you so.

Who says the lover kills the man in me?
  Beneath the day's hot blue
This thing hunts cover and my heart fights
      free
  To laugh an hour or two.
But now it wavers like a wounded doe.
The wind is blowin' and I want you so.

ON BOOT HILL

Up from the prairie and through the pines,
Over your straggling headboard lines
. Winds of the West go by.
You must love them, you booted dead,
More than the dreamers who died in bed—
You old-timers who took your lead
 Under the open sky!

Leathery knights of the dim old trail,
Lawful fighters or scamps from jail,
 Dimly your virtues shine.
Yet who am I that I judge your wars,
Deeds that my daintier soul abhors,
Wide-open sins of the wide outdoors,
 Manlier sins than mine.

Dear old mavericks, customs mend.
I would not glory to make an end
 Marked like a homemade sieve.
But with a touch of your own old pride
Grant me to travel the trail I ride.
Gamely and gaily, the way you died,
 Give me the nerve to live.

Ay, and for you I will dare assume
Some Valhalla of sun and room
   Over the last divide.
There, in eternally fenceless West,
Rest to your souls, if they care to rest,
Or else fresh horses beyond the crest
   And a star-speckled range to ride.

GRASS GROWN TRAILS

THE COYOTE

Trailing the last gleam after,
  In the valleys emptied of light,
Ripples a whimsical laughter
  Under the wings of the night.
Mocking the faded west airily,
Meeting the little bats merrily,
  Over the mesas it shrills
  To the red moon on the hills.

Mournfully rising and waning,
  Far through the moon-silvered land
Wails a weird voice of complaining
  Over the thorns and the sand.
Out of blue silences eerily,
On to the black mountains wearily,
  Till the dim desert is crossed,
  Wanders the cry, and is lost.

Here by the fire's ruddy streamers,
  Tired with our hopes and our fears,
We inarticulate dreamers
  Hark to the song of our years.

Up to the brooding divinity
Far in that sparkling infinity
    Cry our despair and delight,
    Voice of the Western night!

THE FREE WIND

I went and worked in a drippin' mine
    'Mong the rock and the oozin' wood,
For the dark seemed lit with a dollar sign
    And they told me money's good.
So I jumped and sweat for a flat-foot boss
    Till my pocket bulged with pay,
But my heart it fought like a led bronc hawse
    Till I flung my drill away.

For the wind, the wind, the good free wind,
    She sang from the pine divide
That the sky was blue and the young years few
    And the world was big and wide!
From the poor, bare hills all gashed with scars
    I rode till the range was crossed;
Then I watched the gold of sunset bars
And my camp-sparks glintin' toward the stars
    And laughed at the pay I'd lost.

I went and walked in the city way
    Down a glitterin' canyon street,
For the thousand lights looked good and gay
    And they said life there was sweet.

So the wimmen laughed while night reeled by
  And the wine ran red and gold,
But their laugh was the starved wolf's huntin'
    cry
  And their eyes were hard and old.

And the wind, the wind, the clean free wind,
  She laughed through the April rains:
"Come out and live by the wine I give
  In the smell of the greenin' plains!"
And I looked back once to the smoky towers
  Where my face had bleached so pale,
Then loped through the lash of drivin' show-
    ers
To the uncut sod and the prairie flowers
  And the old wide life o' the trail.

I went and camped in the valley trees
  Where the thick leaves whispered rest,
For love lived there 'mong the honey bees,
  And they told me love was best.
There the twilight lanes were cool and dim
  And the orchards pink with May,
Yet my eyes they'd lift to the valley's rim
  Where the desert reached away.

And the wind, the wind, the wild free wind,
  She called from the web love spun
To the unbought sand of the lone trail land
  And the sweet hot kiss o' the sun!
Oh, I looked back twice to the valley lass,
Then I set my spurs and sung,
For the sun sailed up above the pass
And the mornin' wind was in the grass
. And my hawse and me was young.

THE MEDICINE MAN

"The trail is long to the bison herd,
  The prairie rotten with rain,
And look! the wings of the thunder bird
  Blacken the hills again.
A medicine man the gods may balk—
Go fight for us with the thunder hawk!"

The medicine man flung out his arms.
  "I am weary of woman talk
And cook-fire witching and childish charms!
  I fight you the thunder hawk!"
Then he took his arrows and climbed the butte
While the warriors watched him, scared and
      mute.

A wind from the wings began to blow
  And the arrows of rain to shoot,
As the medicine man raised high his bow,
  Standing alone on the butte,
And the day went dark to the cowering band
As the arrow leaped from his steady hand.

For the thunder hawk swooped down to fight
  And who in his way could stand?
The flash of his eye was blinding bright
  And his wing-clap stunned the land.
The braves yelled terror and loosed the rain
And scattered far on the drowning plain.

So, after the thunder hawk swept by,
  They found him, scorched and slain,
Yet (fighting with gods, who fears to die?)
  He smiled with a light disdain.
That smile was glory to all his clan
But none dared touch the medicine man.

THE PIANO AT RED'S

'Twas a hole called Red's Saloon
  In La Vaca town;
'Twas an old piano there,
  Blistered, marred and brown,
And a man more battered still,
  Takin's drinks for fees,
Played all night from memory
  On the yellow keys.

While the glasses clinked and clashed
  On the sloppy bar,
That piano's dreamy voice
  Took you out and far,
Ridin' old, forgotten trails
  Underneath the moon,
Till you heard a drunken yell
  Back in Red's Saloon.

Whirr of wheel and slap of cards,
  Talk of loss and gain,
Mixed with hum of honey bees
  Down a sunny lane.

Glimpses of your mother's face,
  Touch of girlish lips
Often made you lose your count
  As you stacked your chips.

Scufflin' feet and thud of fists,
  Curses hot as fire——
Still the music sang of love,
  Longin', lost desire,
Dreams that never could have been,
  Joys that couldn't stay —
While the man upon the floor
  Wiped the blood away.

Then, some way, it followed you,
  Slept upon your breast,
Trailed you out across the range,
  Never let you rest;
And for days and days you'd hum
  Just one scrap of tune—
Funny place for music, though,
  Back in Red's Saloon!

A RANGER

He never made parade of tooth or claw;
    He was plain as us that nursed the bawlin'
        herds.
Though he had a rather meanin'-lookin' jaw,
    He was shy of exercisin' it with words.
As a circuit-ridin' preacher of the law,
    All his preachin' was the sort that hit the
        nail;
He was just a common ranger, just a ridin'
        pilgrim stranger,
    And he labored with the sinners of the trail.

Once a Yaqui knifed a woman, jealous mad,
    Then hit southward with the old, old kill-
        er's plan,
And nobody missed the woman very bad,
    While they'd just a little rather missed the
        man.
But the ranger crossed his trail and sniffed it
        glad,
    And then loped away to bring him back
        again,

*"The taut ropes sing like a banjo string
And the latigoes creak and strain."*

See page 60

For he stood for peace and order on the
    lonely, sunny border
And his business was to hunt for sinful
    men!

So the trail it led him southward all the day,
    Through the shinin' country of the thorn
      and snake,
Where the heat had drove the lizards from
    their play
    To the shade of rock and bush and yucca
      stake.
And the mountains heaved and rippled far
    away
    And the desert broiled as on the devil's
      prong
But he didn't mind the devil if his head kep'
    clear and level
    And the hoofs beat out their quick and
      steady song.

Came the yellow west, and on far-off rise
    Something black crawled up and dropped
      beyond the rim,

And he reached his rifle out and rubbed his
      eyes
  While he cussed the southern hills for
      growin' dim.
Down a hazy 'royo came the coyote cries,
  Like they laughed at him because he'd lòst
      his mark,
And the smile that brands a fighter pulled his
      mouth a little tighter
  As he set his spurs and rode on through the
     dark.

Came the moonlight on a trail that wriggled
      higher
  Through the mountains that look into
      Mexico,
And the shadows strung his nerves like banjo
      wire
  And the miles and minutes dragged un-
      earthly slow.
Then a black mesquite spit out a thread of fire
  And the canyon walls flung thunder back
      again,

And he caught himself and fumbled at his
    rifle while he grumbled
That his bridle arm had weight enough for
    ten.

Though his rifle pointed wavy-like and slack
    And he grabbed for leather at his hawse's
    shy,
Yet he sent a soft-nosed exhortation back
    That convinced the sinner—just above the
    eye.
So the sinner sprawled among the shadows
    black
    While the ranger drifted north beneath the
    moon,
Wabblin' crazy in his saddle, workin' hard to
    stay astraddle
    While the hoofs beat out a slow and sorry
    tune.

When the sheriff got up early out of bed,
    How he stared and vowed his soul a total
    loss,

As he saw the droopy thing all blotched with
    red
  That came ridin' in aboard a tremblin'
    hawse.
But "I got 'im" was the most the ranger said
  And you couldn't hire him, now, to tell the
    tale;
He was just a quiet ranger, just a ridin' pil-
    grim stranger
  And he labored with the sinners of the trail.

ON THE DRIVE

Oh, days whoop by with swingin' lope
    And days slip by a-sleepin',
And days must drag, with lazy rope,
    Along the trail a-creepin'.
Heeya-a! you cattle; drift away!
Heeyow! the slow hoofs sift away
And sunny dust clouds lift away,
    Along the trail a-creepin'.

My pard may sing of sighin' love
    And I of roarin' battle,
But all the time we sweat and shove
    And follow up the cattle.
Heeya-a! the bawlin' crowd of you!
Heeyow the draggin' cloud of you!
We're glad and gay and proud of you,
    We men that follow cattle!

But all the world's a movin' herd
    Where men drift on together,
And some may spur and some are spurred,
    But most are horns and leather!

Heeya-a! the rider sings along,
Heeyow! the reined hawse swings along
And drifts and drags and flings along
   The mob of horns and leather.

The outlaws fight to break away;
   The weak and lame are crawlin',
But only dead ones quit the play,
   The dust-cloud and the bawlin'.
Heeya-a! it's grief and strife to us;
Heeyow! it's child and wife to us;
By leap or limp, it's life to us;
   The dust-cloud and the bawlin'.

Some dream ahead to pastures green,
   Some stare ahead to slaughter,
But, anyway, night drops between
   And brings us rest and water.
Heeya-a! you cattle, drift away!
Heeyow! the dust-clouds lift away;
The glarin' miles will shift away
   And leave us rest and water.

SATURDAY NIGHT

Out from the ranch on a Saturday night,
 Ridin' a hawse that's a shootin' star,
Close on the flanks of the flyin' daylight,
 Racin' with dark for the J L Bar.
Fox-trot and canter will do for the day;
It's a gallop, my love, when I'm ridin' your
  way.

Up the arroyo the trippin' hoofs beat,
 Flingin' the hinderin' gravel wide;
Now your light glimmers across the mes-
  quite,
 Glimpsed from the top of a rocky divide;
Down through a draw where the shadows are
  gray
I'm comin', my darlin', I'm ridin' your way.

West, where the sky is a-blushin' afar,
 Matchin' your cheeks as the daylight dies,
West, where the shine of a glitterin' star
 Hints of the light I will find in your eyes,

Night-birds are passin' the signal to say:
  "He's comin', my lady, he's ridin' your
    way."

Hoof-beats are measurin' seconds so fast,
  Clickin' them off with an easy rhyme;
Minutes will grow into months at the last,
  Mebbe to bring us a marryin' time.
Life would be singin' and work would be play
If every night I was ridin' your way.

SOUTHWESTERN JUNE

Lazy little hawse, it's noon
   And we've wasted saddle leather,
But the mornin's slip so soon
   When we drift around together
   In this lazy, shinin' weather,
Sunny, easy-goin' June.

Who kin study shamblin' herds,
   How they calve or die or wander,
When the bridegroom mockin'-birds,
   Singin' here and there and yonder,
   Trill that June's too bright to ponder
And life's just too fine for words!

Down the desert's hazy blue
   See the tall gray whirlwinds farin',
Slow, contented sort of crew
   Trailin' 'cross the sunny barren,
   Headed nowhere and not carin'
Just the same as me and you.

From a world of unfenced room
   Just a breath of breeze is strayin',
Triflin' with the yucca bloom

Till its waxy bells are swayin',
On my cheek warm kisses layin'
Soft as touch of ostrich plume.

When the July lightnin' gleams
This brown range will start to workin',
Hills be green and tricklin' streams
Down each deep arroyo lurkin';
Now the sleepy land is shirkin',
Drowzin', smilin' in her dreams.

Steppin' little hawse, it's noon.
Turquoise blue the far hills glimmer;
"Sun—sun—sun," the mockers croon
Where the yellow range lands shimmer,
And our sparklin' spirits simmer
For we're young yet, and it's June!

THE NIGHT HERDER

I laughed when the dawn was a-peepin'
  And swore in the blaze of the noon,
But down from the stars is a-creepin'
  A softer, oneasier tune.
  Away, and away, and away,
  The whisperin' night seems to say
Though the trail-weary cattle are sleepin'
  And the desert dreams under the moon.

By day, if the roarin' herd scatters,
  My heart it is steady and set,
But now, when they're quiet, it patters
  Like the ball in a spinnin' roulette.
  Away, and away, and away
  To the rim where the heat lightnin's play—
Out there is the one trail that matters
  To the valley I never forget.

There's a pass where the black shadows
    shiver,
  Then a desert all silvery blue,
A divide, and the breaks by the river,
  Then a light in the valley—and you!

Away, and away, and away—
'Tis a month till I see you by day,
But under the moon it's forever
    And the weary trail winds the world
        through.

The coyotes are laughin' out yonder,
    A happy owl whoops on the hill—
Oh, wild, lucky things that kin wander
    As far and as free as they will!
    Away, and away, and away,
    And I that am wilder than they
Must loll in my saddle and ponder
    Or sing for the cows to be still!

I see the dark river waves wrinkle;
    The valley trees droop in a swoon;
You're dreamin' where valley bells tinkle
    And half-asleep mockin'-birds croon.
    Away, and away, and away—
    Do your dainty dreams ever stray
To a camp where the desert stars twinkle
    And a lone rider sings to the moon?

HAWSE WORK

Stop! there's the wild bunch to right of the
　　trail,
Heads up and ears up and ready to sail,
Led by a mare with the green in her eyes,
Mean as the devil and nearly as wise.
Circle 'em, boys, and the pass is the place;
Settle your heels for a rowelin' race.

*Oh, hawse work! the sweep and the drift
　　of it!*
Hawse work! the leap and the lift of it!
Who wants to fly in the empty blue sky
　　When he kin ride on the hawse work!

Hi! and they're off in a whirlwind. So!
Straight in the line we don't want 'em to go;
Light-footed, wild-hearted, look at 'em flit!
Head 'em, now! rowel, and turn loose the bit!
Whee! and the rip and the rush and the beat,
Rattlin' rocks and the whippin' mesquite!

*Oh, hawse work! the swing and the swell
　　of it!*
Hawse work! the sing and the yell of it!

Holler goodbye to the dull and the dry;
  Leave 'em behind on the hawse work.

Shorty is down with his hawse in a heap;
Might have pulled in for a gully so deep.
Reddy he rides like he's tired of his life;
Ought to be thinkin' he's got a wife—
Shrinkin' and thinkin' of bones that may
      crunch?
No! Yip! we've headed the mare and her
      bunch!

  Oh, hawse work! the rip and the tear of it!
    Hawse work! the dip and the dare of it!
  Life flutters high when you're lookin' to
      die;
    That is the fun of the hawse work.

Hi! and you're foolish for once, old lass,
Streakin' it straight for the trap in the pass.
Into the canyon the hoof-thunder drums—
Where is that holdup? Hump! there he
      comes,
Crow-hoppin' down from the bluff—too late!
Damn! and they're gone for a tour of the
      State!

Oh, hawse work, the rant and the fuss of it!
  Hawse work! the pant and the cuss of it!
Yet when I sigh and the world is a lie
  Give me a day on the hawse work!

HALF-BREED

Fathers with eyes of ancient ire,
  Old eagles shorn of flight,
Forget the breed of my blue-eyed sire
While I sit this hour by the council fire,
  All red in the fire's red light.

Chant me the day of the war-steed's prance
  And the signal fires on the buttes,
Of the Cheyenne scalps on the lifted lance,
Of the women raped from the Pawnee dance
  And the wild death trail of the Utes.

Sing me the song of the buffalo run
  To the edge of the canyon snare,
With the roaring plunge when the meat was
      won
And the flash of knives in the low red sun
  And the good blood smell in the air.

Chant me the might of the Manitou—
  But the old song drags and dies.
Old things have drifted the sunset through
Till the very God of the land comes new
  From the rim where the young stars rise!

Fathers, red men, the red flame falls,
　And over the dim dawn lands
My white soul hunts me again and calls
To the lanes of law and the shadow of walls
　And a woman with soft white hands.

TO HER

Cut loose a hundred rivers,
   Roaring across my trail,
Swift as the lightning quivers,
   Loud as a mountain gale.
I build me a boat of slivers;
   I weave me a sail of fur,
And ducks may founder and die
     But I
Cross that river to her!

Bunch the deserts together,
   Hang three suns in the vault;
Scorch the lizards to leather,
   Strangle the springs with salt.
I fly with a buzzard feather,
   I dig me wells with a spur,
And snakes may famish and fry
     But I
Cross that desert to her!

Murder my sleep with revel;
   Make me ride through the bogs

Knee to knee with the devil,
　　Just ahead of the dogs.
I harrow the Bad Lands level,
　　I teach the tiger to purr,
For saints may wallow and lie
　　　　But I
　　Go clean-hearted to her!

THE LOCOED HORSE

As I was ridin' all alone
  And winkin' in the noontime glare,
I seen a hawse all hide and bone
  Walk 'round a willow dead and bare—
Walk 'round and 'round, with limp and
      groan,
  And hunt the shade that wasn't there.
And then says I: "That sorry steed
Has been and et the loco weed."

Near by a spreadin' live oak laid
  Its wide, cool shadow on the ground,
But then he knowed that willow's shade
  Was just a little further 'round
And reckoned, each slow step he made,
  That in the next it would be found.
There, like a coon, his thoughts were treed
Since he had et the loco weed.

The water trail went windin' by,
  The sweet brown grass furred every slope
And he was ga'nt and starved and dry,

Yet, on his ghostly picket rope
Led 'round and 'round, he still must try
That hopeless circle of his hope.
He didn't think of drink or feed
Since he had et the loco weed.

A playful wild bunch topped the hill
And stared with eyes all impish bright
And whinnered to him sweet and shrill,
Then flung their heads and loped from
sight,
Yet from that everlastin' mill
They couldn't make him stray a mite.
He never seen their gay stampede
For he had et the loco weed.

When next that range I had to ride
Beneath his willow tree he lay,
Just wornout hoofs and faded hide
And big black birds that flopped away;
But yet I reckon that he died
Still hopeful—happy—who kin say?
Sometimes I think I mostly need
To eat some sort of loco weed.

THE LONG WAY

Two miles of ridin' from the school, without
    a bit of trouble—
  The main road hit her father's ranch as
    straight as you could fall.
I led her by a shorter cut that made the dis-
    tance double
  And guided her along a trail that wasn't
    there at all.

The long way, the long way, but ridin' it to-
    gether
  I never cared a feather for the length and
    never shall,
With happy hoofs that shuffled to the singin'
    saddle leather
  And laughin' wind that ruffled sunny miles
    of chaparral.

The trail of our meanderin' would tire a wolf
    to follow;
  The range was hardly wide enough for us
    to go around.

I dared to hope she liked it, bare hill and
thorny hollow,
And prayed that all her likin' wasn't wasted on the ground.

*The long way, the long way, and down the
wind we drifted,
And soon the sand was sifted in our tracks
and they were gone,
I dreamed of no forgettin' while to me her
face was lifted,
Nor knowed the sun was settin', for her
eyes were full of dawn.*

Perhaps I hoped that we were lost without a
trail to guide us.
It shocked me like a bullet when the dogs
began to bark,
And suddenly, from nowhere, the ranch was
there beside us,
She reined away and left me, and the world
was in the dark.

The long way, the long way, of all my old
    Septembers,
  Gone gray like campfire embers when the
    midnight coyote shrills,
One hour stays golden mellow—do you reckon
    she remembers
  That sunset fadin' yellow through the
    notches of the hills?

FREIGHTIN'

Forty miles from Taggart's store,
    Fifty yet to grind,
Heavin' six strung out before,
    Trailer snubbed behind;
Half a world of glarin' sand
    Prayin' for a tree,
Nothin' movin' 'cross the land
    But the sun and me.

Chuck an' luck! luck an' chuck!
    Grunts the workin' wheels;
Lazy gust swirls up the dust
    From the hawses' heels.
I've been young and raced and sung,
    But I've learnt my load.
Slow, slow, on we go
    Out the stretchin' road.

Where the sky-line waves and breaks
    Shines a misty beach
And the blue of ripplin' lakes—
    Lakes no man kin reach.

Just beyond my leaders' bits
  Winds the life I know,
Ruts and 'royos, hills and pits
  In a daylong row.

Chuck an' luck! luck an' chuck!
  Life's more miss than hit.
Luck's the thing I dream and sing;
  Chuck is all I git!
'Neath the sky I crawl and fry
  Like the horny toad.
Slow, slow, on we go
  Out the stretchin' road.

When I reach that sparklin' line
  Where the ripples run,
There'll be just this road of mine
  And the dust and sun.
Mebbe on my last far hill,
  Where the dream-mist clears,
I'll be freightin', freightin' still
  Down the road of years.

Chuck an' luck! luck an' chuck!
  Sky-lines mostly lie,

© Huffman-Stevenson.

"I wait to hear him ridin' up behind."

See page 84

Yet they beat the limp mesquite
  That goes trailin' by.
Luck enough to move my stuff—
  More I've never knowed.
Slow, slow, on we go
  Out the stretchin' road.

Slim and far our shadow swings;
  Sun is on his knees.
Some one's campin' at the springs—
  Smell it down the breeze.
Chuck time, boys, and sleep besides,
  When we've chomped our hay.
Durn your dusty, trusty hides!
  You've sho' earned your pay.

Chuck an' luck! luck an' chuck!
  Grunts the weary wheels;
Dreams untold and sunset gold,
  Cussin' sweat and meals.
If you kin, Lord, let me win,
  But I'll move my load.
Slow, slow, on we go
  Out the stretchin' road.

THE RAINS

You've watched the ground-hog's shadow and
    the shiftin' weather signs
  Till the Northern prairie starred itse'f with
    flowers;
You've seen the snow a-meltin' up among the
    Northern pines
  And the mountain creeks a-roarin' with the
    showers.
You've blessed the stranger sunlight when the
    Winter days were done
  And the Summer creepin' down the budded
    lanes.
Did you ever see a Springtime in the home
    range of the sun,
  When the desert land is waitin' for the
    Rains?

The April days are sun and sun; the last thin
    cloud is fled.
  It's gold above the eastern mountain crest,
Then blaze upon the yellow range all day
    from overhead
  And then a stripe of gold across the west.

The dry wind mourns among the hills, a-hunt-
    in' trees and grass,
  Then down the desert flats it rises higher
And sweeps a rollin' dust-storm up and flings
    it through the pass
  And fills the evenin' west with smoulderin'
    fire.

It's sun and sun without a change the lazy
    length o' May
  And all the little sun things own the land.
The horned toad basks and swells himse'f;
    the bright swifts dart and play;
  The rattler hunts or dozes in the sand.
The wind comes off the desert like it brushed
    a bed of coals;
  The sickly range grass withers down and
    fails;
The bony cattle bawl around the dryin' water
    holes,
  Then stagger off along the stony trails.
The days crawl on to Summer suns that
    slower blaze and wheel;
  The mesas heave and quiver in the noon.

The mountains they are ashes and the sky is
    shinin' steel,
  Though the mockin'-birds are singin' that
    it's June.
And here and there among the hills, a-stand-
    in' white and tall,
  The droopin' plumes of yucca flowers
    gleam,
The buzzards circle, circle where the starvin'
    cattle fall
  And the whole hot land seems dyin' in a
    dream.
But last across the sky-line comes a thing
    that's strange and new,
  A little cloud of saddle blanket size.
It blackens 'long the mountains and bulges up
    the blue
  And shuts the weary sun-glare from our
    eyes.
Then the lightnin's gash the heavens and the
    thunder jars the world
  And the gray of fallin' water wraps the
    plains,

And 'cross the burnin' ranges, down the
    wind, the word is whirled:
  "Here's another year of livin', and the
    Rains!"
You've seen your fat fields ripplin' with the
    treasure that they hoard;
  Have you seen a mountain stretch and rub
    its eyes?
Or bare hills lift their streamin' faces up and
    thank the Lord,
  Fairly tremblin' with their gladness and
    surprise?
Have you heard the 'royos singin' and the new
    breeze hummin' gay,
  As the greenin' ranges shed their dusty
    stains—
Just a whole dead world sprung back to life
    and laughin' in a day!
  Did you ever see the comin' of the Rains?

THE BORDER

When the dreamers of old Coronado,
   From the hills where the heat ripples run,
Made a dust to the far Colorado
   And wagged their steel caps in the sun,
They prayed like the saint and the martyr
   And swore like the devils below,
For a man is both angel and Tartar
   In the land where the dry rivers flow.

Ay, the Border, the sun smitten Border,
   That fences the Land of the Free,
Where the desert glares grim like a warder
   And the Rio gleams on to the sea;
Where ruins, like dreamy old sages,
Hint tales of dead empires and ages,
Where a young race is rearing the stages
   Of ambitious empires to be.

Came the padres to soften the savage
   And show him the heavenly goal;
Came Spaniards to piously ravage
   And winnow his flesh from his soul;

Then miner and riotous herder,
　　Over-riding white breed of the North,
Brought progress, and new sorts of murder,
　　And a kind of perpetual Fourth.

Ay, the Border, the whimsical Border,
　　Deep purples and dazzling gold,
Soft hearts full of mirthful disorder,
　　Hard faces, sun wrinkled and old,
Warm kisses 'neath patio roses,
Cold lead as the luck-god disposes,
Clean valor fame never discloses,
　　Black trespasses laughingly told!

Then out from the peaceful old places
　　Walked the Law, grave, strong and serene,
And the harsh elbow-rub of the races
　　Was padded, with writs in between.
Then stilled was the strife and the racket
　　That neighborly love might advance—
With a knife in the sleeve of its jacket
　　And a gun in the band of its pants.

Ay, the Border, the bright, placid Border!
　　It sleeps, like a snake in the sun,

Like a "hole" tamped and primed in due or-
    der,
  Like a shining and full throated gun.
But the dust-devil dances and staggers
And the yucca flower daintily swaggers
At her birth from a cluster of daggers,
  And ever the heat ripples run.

Fierce, hot, is the Border's bright daytime,
  Calm, sweet, the vast night on its plains;
White hell on the mesas, its Maytime,
  A green-and-gold heaven, its Rains.
It is grimmer than slumber's dark brother,
  'Tis as gay as the mocking-bird likes;
It loves like a lioness mother
  And strikes as the rattlesnake strikes.

Ay, the Border, bewildering Border,
  Our youngest, and oldest, domains,
Where the face of the Angel Recorder
  Knits hard between chuckles and pains,
Vast peace, the clear sky's earthly double,
Witch cauldron forever a-bubble,
Home of mystery, splendor and trouble
  And a people with sun in their veins.

THE BAD LANDS

No fresh green things in the Bad Lands bide;
  It is all stark red and gray,
And strewn with bones that had lived and
      died
  Ere the first man saw the day.
When the sharp crests dream in the sunset
      gleam
  And the bat through the canyon veers,
You will sometimes catch, if you listen long,
The tones of the Bad Lands' mystic song,
  A song of a million years.

The place is as dry as a crater cup,
  Yet you hear, as the stars shine free,
From the barren gulches sounding up,
  The lap of a spawning sea,
A breeze that cries where the great ferns rise
  From the pools on a new-made shore,
With the whip and whir of batlike wings
And the snarl of slimy, fighting things
  And the tread of the dinosaur.

Then the sea voice ebbs through untold morns,
    And the jungle voices reign—
The hunting howl and the clash of horns
    And the screech of rage and pain.
Harsh and grim is the old earth hymn
    In that far brute paradise,
And as ages drift the rough strains fall
To a single note more grim than all,
    The crack of the glacial ice.

So the song runs on, with shift and change,
    Through the years that have no name,
And the late notes soar to a higher range,
    But the theme is still the same.
Man's battle-cry and the guns' reply
    Blend in with the old, old rhyme
That was traced in the score of the strata
       marks
While millenniums winked like campfire
       sparks
    Down the winds of unguessed time.

There's a finer fight than of tooth and claw,
    More clean than of blade and gun,

But, fair or foul, by the Great Bard's law
   'Twill be fight till the song is done.
Not mine to sigh for the song's deep "why,"
   Which only the Great Bard hears.
My soul steps out to the martial swing
Of the brave old song that the Bad Lands
     sing,
   The song of a million years.

THE SPRINGTIME PLAINS

Heart of me, are you hearing
The drum of hoofs in the rains?
Over the Springtime plains I ride
Knee to knee with Spring
And glad as the summering sun that comes
Galloping north through the zodiac!
Heart of me, let's forget
The plains death white and still,
When lonely love through the stillness called
Like a smothered stream that sings of Summer
Under the snow on a Winter night.
Now the frost is blown from the sky
And the plains are living again.
Lark lovers sing on the sunrise trail,
Wild horses call to me out of the noon,
Watching me pass with impish eyes,
Gray coyotes laugh in the quiet dusk
And the plains are glad all day with me.
Heart of me, all the way
My heart and the hoofs keep time,
And the wide, sweet winds from the greening
     world

Shout in my ears a glory song,
For nearer, nearer, mile and mile,
Over the quivering rim of the plains,
Is the valley that Spring and I love best
And the waiting eyes of you!

ON THE OREGON TRAIL

We're the prairie pilgrim crew,
  Sailin' with the sun,
Lookin' West to meet a great reward,
Trailin' toward a land that's new
  Like our fathers done,
Trustin' in our rifles and the Lord.

    A-ll set! Go ahead!
    Out the prairie trail.
Leave the woods and settlements behind.
  Trail and settle, work and fight
  Till the rollin' earth is white,—
That's the law and gospel of our kind.

Desert suns and throats o' dust,
  But we never stop;
Wimmin-folks are knittin' as they ride.
We're a breed that, when we must,
  Fight until we drop,
But our work and git-thar is our pride.

    A-ll set! Go ahead!
    Up the sandy Platte.
Leave the circle smokin' in the dawn,

So the comin' hosts will know,
'Mongst the trails of buffalo
Where their darin' brother whites have gone.

Night so black 'twould blind a fox,
    Yells and feathered sleet,
Aim the best you kin and trust to luck.
Arrows whang the wagon box
    But all hell kain't beat
Rifles from Missoury and Kentuck.

A-ll set! Go ahead!
    Leave the dead to sleep
Till the desert sees the Judgment Day.
    Mourn the good boys laid so low,
    But we'll mourn them on the go—
Pawnee! Ogalalla! Cl'ar the way!

Far across the glarin' plain
    See the mountain peaks
Glimmer 'long the edge like flecks o' foam.
Shove! you oxen, till your chain
    Stretches out and squeaks;
Somewhere out beyond that range is *Home!*

A-ll set!' Go ahead!
  Trailin' toward the West
Till the sunset's shinin' flag is furled.
  Ay, our flag's the Western skies,
  Flag that drew our fathers' eyes,
Flag that leads the white man 'round the
    world.

THE FOREST RANGERS

Red is the arch of the nightmare sky,
　Red are the mountains beneath,
Bright where a million red imps leap high,
　Dancing and snapping their teeth.

A keen fight! a clean fight!
　Shoulder your shovels and follow
Up, while they stop in the pines at the top,
　Shooting their sparks in showers.
Up, with your hats ducking under the smoke
　　of it,
Next to the scorch of it, into the choke of it!
　Fight for the ranch in the hollow.
　Fight! for it is not ours.

Why are we fighting from dark to day,
　From summit to canyon wall?
Twice for the Service, and once the pay—
　Most, the hot fun of it all!

A stand fight! a grand fight!
　Into the smother we wallow,

*Stopping their march where the ridge pines
parch
Over the shriveling flowers.
Stick! with the smoke streaming out of the
coats of you,
Sweat in the eyes of you, fire in the throats
of you!
Fight for the ranch in the hollow.
Fight! for it is not ours.*

THE YELLOW STUFF

By the rim rocks on the hill
   The canyon side is rifted
Where Grasping Gabe, with pick and drill,
   Once mucked and shot and drifted.
His hairy arms were never still;
   His eyes were never lifted.

The yellow stuff! The yellow stuff!
   All day his steel would tinkle
And when the blast roared out at last
   He scanned each rocky wrinkle.
That tunnel's face was life to him,
And joy and kids and wife to him
   Its thread of yellow twinkle.

By the rim rocks where he wrought
   A wall that looked eternal
Caved in one day and Gabe was caught
   Snug as a walnut kernel,
Shut up with hunger, thirst and thought
   In dark that was infernal.

The yellow stuff! The yellow stuff!
  Then Gabe forgot its uses,
And all the gold the hills could hold
  Looked like a pair of deuces.
No joy was dust and ore to him;
The gold outside was more to him
  That slanted through the spruces.

By the rim rocks, far away
  From helpers or beholders,
Gabe worked a lifetime in a day,
  Then shoved out head and shoulders
And cried and kissed the light that lay
  Upon the sunny boulders.

The yellow stuff! The yellow stuff!
  He blessed the sunset shining,
Too high in grade to be assayed
  And pure beyond refining.
What scum his work had doled to him,
When God would give such gold to him
  Without a lick of mining!

THE SHEEP-HERDER

All day across the sagebrush flat
   Beneath the sun of June,
My sheep they loaf and feed and blat
   Their never changin' tune.
And then at night time, when they lay
   As quiet as a stone,
I hear the gray wolf far away;
   "Alo-one!" he says, "Alo-one!"

A-a! m-a! ba-a! eh-eh-eh!
   The tune the woollies sing;
It's rasped my ears, it seems, for years,
   Though really just since spring;
And nothin', far as I kin see
   Around the circle's sweep,
But sky and plains, my dreams and me
   And them infernal sheep.

I've got one book—it's poetry—
   A bunch of pretty wrongs
An Eastern lunger gave to me;
   He said 'twas "shepherd songs."

But though that poet sure is deep
  And has sweet things to say,
He never seen a herd of sheep,
  Or smelt them, anyway.

A-a! ma-a! ba-a! eh-eh-eh!
  My woollies greasy gray,
An awful change has hit the range
  Since that old poet's day.
For you're just silly, on'ry brutes
  And I look like distress
And my pipe ain't the kind that toots
  And there's no "shepherdess."

Yet 'way down home in Kansas State,
  Bliss Township, Section Five,
There's one that promised me to wait,
  The sweetest girl alive.
That's why I salt my wages down
  And mend my clothes with strings,
While others blow their pay in town
  For booze and other things.

A-a! ma-a! ba-a! eh-eh-eh!
  My Minnie, don't be sad;

Next year we'll lease that splendid piece
  That corners on your dad.
We'll drive to "literary," dear,
  The way we used to do
And turn my lonesome workin' here
  To happiness for you.

Suppose, down near that rattlers' den,
  While I sit here and dream,
I'd see a bunch of ugly men
  And hear a woman scream.
Suppose I'd let my rifle shout
  And drop the men in rows,
And then the woman should turn out—
  My Minnie!—just suppose.

A-a! ma-a! ba-a! eh-eh-eh!
  The tune would then be gay;
There is, I mind, a parson kind
  Just forty miles away.
Why Eden would come back again
  With sage and sheep corrals,
And I could swing a singin' pen
  To write her "pastorals."

I pack a rifle on my arm
 And jump at flies that buzz;
There's nothin' here to do me harm
 I sometimes wish there was.
If through that brush above the pool
 A 'red should creep—and creep—
Wah! cut down on 'im! Stop, you fool!
 That's nothin' but a sheep.

A-a! ma-a! ba-a!—Hell!
 Oh, sky and plain and bluff!
Unless my mail comes up the trail
 I'm locoed, sure enough.
What's that?—a dust-whiff near the butte
 Right where my last trail ran,
A movin' speak, a—wagon! Hoot!
 Thank God! here comes a man.

THE OLD PROSPECTOR

There's a song in the canyon below me
  And a song in the pines overhead,
As the sunlight crawls down from the snow-
      line
And rustles the deer from his bed.
With mountains of green all around me
  And mountains of white up above
And mountains of blue down the sky-line,
  I follow the trail that I love.

My hands they are hard from the shovel,
  My leg is rheumatic by streaks
And my face it is wrinkled from squintin'
  At the glint of the sun on the peaks.
You pity the prospector sometimes
  As if he was out of your grade.
Why, you are all prospectors, bless you!
  I'm only a branch of the trade.
You prospect for wealth and for wisdom,
  You prospect for love and for fame;
Our work don't just match as to details,
  But the principle's mostly the same.

While I swing a pick in the mountains
  You slave in the dust and the heat
And scratch with your pens for a color
  And assay the float of the street.

You wail that your wisdom is salted,
  That fame never pays for the mill,
That wealth hasn't half enough value
  To pay you for climbin' the hill.
You even say love's El Dorado,
  A pipe dream that never endures—
Well, my luck ain't all that I want it,
  But I never envied you yours.
You're welcome to what the town gives you,
  To prizes of laurel and rose,
But leave me the song in the pine tops,
  The breath of a wind from the snows.
With mountains of green all around me
  And mountains of white up above
And mountains of blue down the sky-line,
  I'll follow the trail that I love.

© Huffman-Stevenson.

"There's land where yet no ditches dig
Nor cranks experiment;
It's only lovely, free and big
And isn't worth a cent."

See page 93

GOD OF THE OPEN

God of the open, though I am so simple
   Out in the wind I can travel with you,
Noons when the hot mesas ripple and dimple,
   Nights when the stars glitter cool in the
     blue.
Too far you stand for the reach of my hand,
   Yet I can feel your big heart as it beats
Friendly and warm in the sun or the storm.
   Are you the same as the God of the streets?

Yours is the sunny blue roof I ride under;
   Mountain and plain are the house you have
     made.
Sometimes it roars with the wind and the
     thunder
   But in your house I am never afraid.
He? Oh, they give him the license to live,
   Aim, in their ledgers, to pay him his due,
Gather by herds to present him with words—
   Words! What are words when my heart
     talks with you?

God of the open, forgive an old ranger
  Penned among walls where he never sees
    through.
Well do I know, though their God seems a
    stranger,
  Earth has no room for another like you.
Shut out the roll of the wheels from my soul;
  Send me a wind that is singing and sweet
Into this place where the smoke dims your
    face.
  Help me see you in the God of the street.

THE PASSING OF THE TRAIL

There was a sunny, savage land
  Beneath the eagle's wings,
And there, across the thorns and sand,
  Wild rovers rode as kings.
Is it a yarn from long ago
  And far across the sea?
Could that land be the land we know?
  Those roving riders we?

The trail's a lane, the trail's a lane.
  How comes it, pard of mine?
Within a day it slipped away
  And hardly left a sign.
Now history a tale has gained
  To please the younger ears—
A race of kings that rose, and reigned,
  And passed in fifty years!

Dream back beyond the cramping lanes
  To glories that have been—
The camp smoke on the sunset plains,
  The riders loping in:

Loose rein and rowelled heel to spare,
　The wind our only guide,
For youth was in the saddle there
　With half a world to ride.

The trail's a lane, the trail's a lane.
　Dead is the branding fire.
The prairies wild are tame and mild,
　All close-corralled with wire.
The sunburnt demigods who ranged
　And laughed and lived so free
Have topped the last divide, or changed
　To men like you and me.

Where, in the valley fields and fruits,
　Now hums a lively street,
We milled a mob of fighting brutes
　Among the grim mesquite.
It looks a far and fearful way—
　The trail from Now to Then—
But time is telescoped to-day,
　A hundred years in ten.

The trail's a lane, the trail's a lane.
　Our brows are scarcely seamed,

But we may scan a mighty span
  Methuselah ne'er dreamed.
Yet, pardner, we are dull and old,
  With paltry hopes and fears,
Beside those rovers gay and bold
  Far riding down the years!

LATIGO TOWN

You and I settled this section together;
  Youthful and mettled and wild were we
    then.
You were the gladdest town out in the
    weather;
  I was the maddest young scamp among
    men.

  Latigo Town, ay, Latigo Town,
  Child of the mesa sun-flooded and brown,
That hour of gracious romance and good
    leather,
  Splendid, audacious, comes never, again.

Many a rover as brash as a sparrow,
  Loping in over the amethyst plains,
Reined for your spinning roulette and your
    faro,
  Light-hearted sinning and fiddled refrains.

  Latigo Town, ay, Latigo Town,
  We made a past you are still living down,
Keen for a tussle, with salt in our marrow,
  Steel in our muscles and sun in our veins!

Rowels that jingled and rigs that were tat-
    tered,
    Yet how we tingled to dreams that were
      high!
Slim was the treasure we gathered and scat-
    tered,
    But can you measure the wind and the sky?

    Latigo Town, ay, Latigo Town,
    Freedom and youth were a robe and a
      crown.
Then we were bosses of riches that mattered,
    Laughing at losses of things you can buy.

Town that was fiery and careless and Spanish,
    Boy that was wiry and wayward and glad—
Over the border to limbo they vanish;
    Progress and order decreed they were bad.

    Latigo Town, ay, Latigo Town,
    Pursy with culture and civic renown,
Never censorious progress can banish
    Dreams of the glorious youth that we had!

THE BUFFALO TRAIL

Deeply the buffalo trod it
  Beating it barren as brass;
Now the soft rain-fingers sod it,
  Green to the crest of the pass.
Backward it slopes into history;
Forward it lifts into mystery.
    Here is but wind in the grass.

Backward the millions assemble,
  Bannered with dust overhead,
Setting the prairie a-tremble
  Under the might of their tread.
Forward the sky-line is glistening
And to the reach of our listening
    Drifts not a sound from the dead.

Quick, or swift seasons fade it!
  Look on his works while they show.
This is the bison. He made it.
  Thus say the old ones who know.
This is the bison—a-pondering
Vague as the prairie wind wandering
    Over the green or the snow.

THE CAMP FIRE'S SONG

I reared your fathers long ago—
   Big, savage children—from the breast,
But in the circle of my glow
   You sit to-night a haughty guest,
For far beyond their artless day
Your lofty trail has stretched away.
   So wise! so wise!
But still the child is in your eyes.

Your fathers feared the club and claw,
   Their days were full of fight and flight;
Behind you stands your mighty law
   To guard your lonely sleep to-night,
Or, if some lawless brute run free,
A rifle gleams across your knee.
   So strong! so wise!
But still the fear is in your eyes.

They filled their little tents with spoil,
   Then vaguely longed for greater things;
Your shining cities spurn the soil
   And through your valleys plenty sings;

You span the seas they endless deemed
And rule a world they never dreamed.
　So great! so wise!
But still their longing in your eyes.

They made them gods of flood and fire;
　With simple awe they watched the stars;
You bend all powers to your desire;
　The river gods must draw your cars,
The drudging fire gods drive your fleets,
The lightning slaves about your streets.
　So proud! so wise!
Yet their old wonder in your eyes!

They dreamed a god might in them dwell
　Who lived beyond the silenced heart;
You know your mortal self so well—
　A wondrous thing in every part,
But earthbound as this gaunt mesquite
Or firelit dust about your feet.
　So hard! so wise!
But still the god is in your eyes.

Poor little primal thing am I,
　Great stranger, yet I mock your lore;

Your thickest volumes often lie
   And these still stars could tell you more,
The wind that sighs across the sand
Or I, but could you understand?
   So wise! so wise!
A puzzled child within your eyes.

NEW POEMS

PLAINS BORN

Westward from the greener places
   Where the rivers glint and twine
Stretch the gold-and-purple spaces
   Of the country that is mine;
And to lilac Rockies lifting
   Toward the deeper blue above,
There is neither flaw nor shifting
   In the title of my love.

My own! my own!
Many a silent, sunny zone,
   With the soft cloud shadows drifting
On the desert and the sown!

I would have no wall or warder
   Mar my goodly heritage,
From the yuccas of the border
   To the snowy northern sage—
Glad of every wind that passes
   Down the mesa and the plain,
Singing freedom in the grasses
   And my pony's rippling mane.

My own! my own!
There is freedom here alone,
    Under midnight's starry masses
Or the day king on his throne!

Faith must blunder on in blinkers
    Through a city's swirling rout,
For the milling herd of thinkers
    Blurs the way of wisdom out;
But where stainless sky is bending
    Over never-furrowed sod
There's an open trail ascending
    To the presence of a God!

My own! my own!
Where the troubled eyes are shown
    Heaven and earth forever blending
Round the blue rim of the known!

THE OLD CAMP COFFEE-POT

Written for Eben W. Martin

Old camp-mate, black and rough to see,
A hard-worked aid and ally you
In all my single-handed wars
    With naked nature's savagery.
    Your scars are marks of service true,
    Dear loving-cup of out-o'-doors,
And history in every spot
Has battered you, old coffee-pot.

Oh, black Pandora-box of dreams!
Though dry of drink for mortal needs,
Out of your spout what fancies flow!
    The flash of trout in sunny streams,
    The swoop of ducks among the reeds,
    The buck that paws the reddened snow—
What suns and storms, what dust and mire,
What gay, tanned faces round the fire!

So, vividly as clouds that blaze
Above a sunset's rainy red,
Scene after scene, you bring to me
    The camps and trails of other days.

And as a shell, long dry and dead,
Holds echoes of its native sea,
So dear old murmurs, half forgot,
Rise from your depths, old coffee-pot.

I hear the stir of horses' hoofs,
The solemn challenge of the owl,
The wind song on the piny height,
The lilt of rain on canvas roofs,
The far-off coyote's hungry howl,
And all the camp sounds of the night.
They rise—a thousand things like these—
From you, old well of memories.

Our fires are dead on hill and plain
And old camp faces lost and gone,
But yet we two are left, old friend.
And as the summers bloom and wane
May I meet you at dusk and dawn
By many fires before the end,
And drink to you in nectar hot
From your black throat, old coffee-pot.

MY ENEMY

All mornin' in the mesa's glare
After his crouchin' back I clattered,
And quick shots cut the heavy air
And on the rocks the hot lead spattered.
A dollar crimped, a word too free—
My enemy! My enemy!

He reined beside a rattlers' den
And faced me there to fix the winnin'.
And I wished that he would turn again,
For it was hard to kill him grinnin'.
His hands were empty, I could see.
My enemy! My enemy!

He pointed up; he pointed back.
I looked, and half forgot my hatin'.
A coyote sneaked along our track,
A buzzard hung above us, waitin'.
"Are us four all akin?" says he.
My enemy! My enemy!

The coyote crossed the desert's rim,
The buzzard circled up and faded.

I halved my only smoke with him
And when dark found us limp and jaded,
He sat and kep' the fire for me,
My enemy! My enemy!!

THE FIGHTING SWING

Once again the regiments marching down the
    street,
    Shoulders, legs and rifle barrels swinging
      all in time.
Let the slack civilian plod; ours the gayer
    feet,
    Dancing to the music of the oldest earthly
      rhyme.

Left! Right! Trim and tight, hear the ca-
    dence fall.
    (So the legion Caesar loved shook the
    plains of Gaul.)
Fighting bloods of all the earth in our pulses
    ring.
    Step, lads, true to the dads! Back to the
    fighting swing!

We have kissed goodbye to care, left the fret
    and stew.
    Now the crows may steal the corn; now
    the milk may spill.

All the worries in the world simmer down to
    two—
  One is how to dodge the shells; one is how
    to kill.

Left! Right! Glints of light—down the lines
    they run.
  (So the Janizary spears caught the desert
    sun.)
Once again the fighting steel has its ancient
    fling—
  Flash! sway! battle array. Back to the
    fighting swing!

Every eye is hard and straight; every head
    is high.
  Groping, wrangling days are done; let the
    leaders lead.
Regulations how to live, orders when to die—
  Life and death in primer print any man
    can read.

Left! Right! Eat and fight! Dreams are
  blown to bits.

*(Here's the Old Guard back to life, bound
        for Austerlitz.)*
*Drop the soft and quit the sweet; loose the
        arms that cling.*
*Blood, dust, grapple and thrust—back to
        the fighting swing!*

THE SMOKE-BLUE PLAINS

Kissed me from the saddle and I still can
 feel it burning,
  But he must have felt it cold, for ice was
  in my veins.
I shall always see him as he waved above the
 turning,
  Riding down the canyon to the smoke-blue
  plains.
Oh, the smoke-blue plains! how I used to
 watch them sleeping,
  Thinking peace had dimmed them with the
  shadow of her wings;
Now their gentle haze will seem a smoke of
 death a-creeping,
  Drifted from the battles in the country of
  the kings.

Joked me to the last, and in a voice without a
 quaver—
  Man o' mine!—but underneath the tan his
  cheek was pale.
Never did the nation breed a kinder or a
 braver
  Since our fathers landed from the long sea
  trail.

Oh, the long sea trail he must leave me here
    and follow—
  He that never saw a ship—to dare its
    chances blind,
Out the deadly reaches where the sinking
    steamers wallow.
  Back to trampled countries that his fathers
    left behind.

Down beyond the plains among the fighting
    and the dying,
  God must watch his reckless foot and fol-
    low where it lights;
Guard the places where his blessed tousled
    head is lying—
  Head my shoulder pillowed through the
    warm, safe nights!
Oh, the warm, safe nights, and the pines
    above the shingles!
  Can I stand their crooning and the patter
    of the rains?
Oh, the sunny quiet, and a bridle bit that
    jingles,
  Coming up the canyon from the smoke-
    blue plains!

OTHERS

The daybreak comes so pure and still,.
   He said that I was pure as dawn,
That day we climbed to Signal Hill,
   Back there before the war came on.
God keep me pure as he is brave,
   And fit to take his name.
I let him go and fight to save
   Some other girl from shame.

Across the gulch it glimmers white,
   The little house we plotted for.
We would be sitting there tonight
   If he had never gone to war—
The firelight and the cricket's cheep,
   My arm around his neck—
I let him go and fight to keep
   Some other home from wreck.

And every day I ride to town
   The wide lands talk to me of him—
The slopes with pine trees marching down,
   The spread-out prairies, blue and dim.

"When the last free trail is a prim, fenced lane
And our graves grow weeds through forgetful Mays,
Richer and statelier then you'll reign,
Mother of men whom the world will praise.
And your sons will love you and sigh for you,
Labor and battle and die for you,
But never the fondest will understand
The way we have loved you, young, young land."

See page 97

He loved it for the freedom's sake
  Almost as he loved me.
I let him go and fight to make
  Some other country free.

JEFF HART

Jeff Hart rode out of the gulch to war
  When the low sun yellowed the pines.
He waved to his folks in the cabin door
  And yelled to the men at the mines.
The gulch kept watch till he dropped from
      sight—
Neighbors and girl and kin.
Jeff Hart rode out of the gulch one night;
  Next morning the world came in.

His dad went back to the clinking drills
  And his mother cooked for the men;
The pines branched black on the eastern hills,
  Then black to the west again.
But never again, by dusk or dawn,
  Were the days in the gulch the same,
For back up the trail Jeff Hart had gone
  The trample of millions came.

Then never a clatter of dynamite
  But echoed the guns of the Aisne,
And the coyote's wail in the woods at night
  Was bitter with Belgium's pain.

We heard the snarl of a savage sea
   In the pines when the wind went through,
And the strangers Jeff Hart fought to free
   Grew folks to the folks he knew.

Jeff Hart has drifted for good and all,
   To the ghostly bugles blown,
But the far French valley that saw him fall
   Blood kin to the gulch is grown;
And his foreign folks are ours by right—
   The friends that he died to win.
Jeff Hart rode out of the gulch one night;
   Next morning the world came in.

BATTLE

Do you mind that old fight in The Rattles,
   Whether sheep or cattle men should rule?
Was it that, or was it like most battles—
   Just a drink too many, or a fool?
Anyhow, we all were feelin' funny,
   Strong with lopin' weeks of wind and sun,
Gay, for every hand was full of money,
   Safe, for every sinner packed a gun.
Hi! My! We know it, you and I—
   'Twas safer in the days we packed a gun.

Seems to me that Hell bulged up from under
   Through the floor, volcano-like, and
      broke—
Spits of leaded lightnin' with its thunder,
   Swearin' imps a-whirlin' through the
      smoke—
Dodgin', shootin' fast as they were able,
   Glass and flyin' splinters in a spray—
I was jammed behind a poker table,
   So I had to pull and blaze away.
Hi! My! Who of us thought to die?
   All we knowed was pull and blaze away.

So we had a rippin' roarin' revel
  With the red firewater of the kill,
Dancin' to the pipin' of the devil—
  Then the time arrived to pay the bill.
Bud and Pecos, one across the other,
  Dead below the bluish powder swirls.
Bud, that sent his money to his mother!
  Pecos, with the pigtailed little girls!
Hi! My! I always wonder why
  The bill must go to mother and the girls!

IN THE HILLS

The shadow crawls up canyon walls; the rim
    rocks flush to pink
  A sleepy night hawk lurches up among the
    pines to soar,
And we can hear a thirsty deer tiptoeing
    down to drink - '
  Among the glimmering birches on the hazy
    canyon floor.
Sister, sister, it seems a staring pity—
  Somewhere there is a city, and one time
    there was a war.

Around the bend the thickets end in field and
    garden spot,
  And little ranches lifting smokes that make
    the twilight sweet.
Beneath the smokes the women folks are
    watching pan and pot,
  While joking men are drifting in to smell
    the sizzling meat.
Sister, sister, and is it truth or lying
  That somewhere folks are dying for the
    want of things to eat?

Along the hill the winds are still, and still,
    blue shadows rise,
  And quiet bats are winging out, but down
    the canyon floor
The swift creek purls in dusky swirls that
    mind me of your eyes
  And keeps the stillness singing here for
    ever, evermore.
Sister, sister, and is it true, I wonder—
  Somewhere the loud streets thunder, and
    one time there was a war.

CPSIA information can be obtained
at www.ICGtesting.com
Printed in the USA
BVHW041124071020
590512BV00006B/74